HARDPRESS.NET
HOME OF HARD-TO-FIND BOOKS

A New Translation With Notes, of the Third Satire of Juvenal
by Juvenal

Address:
HardPress
8345 NW 66TH ST #2561
MIAMI FL 33166-2626
USA
Email: info@hardpress.net

THIRD SATIRE

OF

JUVENAL,

S. GOULD, PRINTER.

A

NEW TRANSLATION

WITH NOTES,

OF

THE THIRD SATIRE

OF

JUVENAL.

TO WHICH ARE ADDED,

MISCELLANEOUS POEMS,

ORIGINAL AND TRANSLATED.

NEW-YORK :—PRINTED FOR E. SARGEANT, NO. 39 WALL-STREET, OPPOSITE THE UNITED-STATES BANK.

1806.

CONTENTS.

LETTER FROM A FRIEND.

MY DEAR FRIEND,

  When you imparted to me your defign of publifh-
ing a volume of poems, it occurred to my mind that
the ftyle of your poetry would not be conformable to
the poetical tafte which appears to be now prevalent.
In confequence of this thought, I fuggefted to you
the expediency of prefixing to your book a few pre-
liminary reflections upon the condition of American
poetry; by which it might appear that you were confcious of your departure from the ufual track of your
poetical brethren; and that although you tranfgreffed
the American laws of verfe, your conduct did not proceed from a contempt for all pofitive regulations, but for
fuch only as contravene the everlafting laws of reafon.
Although you were fenfible of the propriety of fuch
an introduction to your mifcellany, you complained
that a want of leifure prevented you from executing
the defign, and requefted me to undertake the per-

formance in your ftead. It would be affectation to
detain you with proteftations of the unwillingnefs and
diffidence with which I at length entered upon the
tafk. With regard to inclination; I was prompted
to comply with your requeft, not only by the defire
of ferving a friend, but by the hope of lending fome
affiftance towards checking an increafing evil. And
as to my want of ability to perform the tafk enjoin-
ed; I was encouraged to hope that the feeblenefs
of my powers would be in fome meafure compenfa-
ted by the goodnefs of my caufe.

I originally intended to notice in a curfory manner the principal productions of our American mufe,
and to point out the leading features in each. But
when I was preparing to execute my plan, two con-
fiderations arofe to prevent me from proceeding in the
manner propofed; the firft was, that almoft all the
productions which compofed our body poetic, bore
fo ftrong a family likenefs to one another, that it
would be an unprofitable wafte of time to enter into a particular defcription of each individual. The
fecond preventing confideration was, that many of the
moft refpectable productions had long fince been dead,
and that it would bear the appearance of irreverent
malignity to call up from their reft thofe who had
fo long been buried in oblivion. The conqueft of
Canaan, Greenfield-Hill, M'Fingal, The Vifion of

Columbus, The Progress of Genius, and others which might be cited, lived very harmlessly, and suffered little injury; they offended no one, and no person felt disposed to offer violence to them; and as they lived peaceably, so they died quietly. Let us not therefore presume to trouble their repose. One general character appears to be stampt upon almost all American poetical productions, they seem to be the offspring of minds faintly glowing with the fire of genius, and unprovided with large stores of wisdom acquired by literary research or extensive observation of mankind.

Nor should it be a subject of any surprise, that our country has risen to no great eminence in poetry; the vast field for productive industry which is open to the great body of the community, prevents much attention even to the most useful learning; no wonder therefore that the ornamental parts of literature are neglected. The grandeur of all the natural objects which meet the eye in our country is certainly favourable to the poetic emotions of an ardent mind; and no doubt, had the indications of poetic genius, which must have appeared on various occasions among us, met with as generous encouragement as has been bestowed upon the genius for painting which some of our countrymen have displayed, America would have been as much distinguished by the eminence of her poets as of her painters.

But though I feel fo much deference for the *Fathers* of American poetry; far different are the emotions which are excited in my breaft by a modern fet of minftrels who are now thrumming their ill-tuned harps, and pouring forth their unmeaning ftrains among us, with increafing applaufe. The tafte of our city in particular appears to be growing every day more vitiated with regard to poetry; thofe verfes are here moft likely to gain admiration which approach neareft to the ftyle of Della Crufca and Anna Matilda, if we except thofe which fome occafional circumftance renders interefting to the public. There is a difficulty attending every attempt to criticife thefe late productions, of the fame nature with that which prevents the demonftration of an axiom; they are fo felf-evidently bad that one is at a lofs for more evident data by the aid of which their badnefs may be proved. Yet effufions of this kind, of various lengths, are daily heard and publicly applauded. To illuftrate what has been afferted, I will adduce two or three examples of the poetry in queftion, which have received the higheft encomiums; and notwithftanding the difficulty of preventing them from eluding, like water, the critical grafp, I will endeavour to examine their boafted beauties, and fet forth their true merits.

There appeared a poem fome time ago, called "The Power of Solitude," which has paffed through two editions, which was highly extolled in one of our public prints, for feveral days fucceffively ; and which had a tolerably extenfive fale in our city. The firft part begins in this ftrain :

" O'er the dim glen when autumn's dewy ray
Sheds the mild luftres of retiring day,
While fcarce the breeze with whifpering murmur
  flows
To hymn its dirge at evening's placid clofe :
When awful filence holds her fullen reign,
And moonlight fparkles on the dimpled main ;
Or thro' fome ancient, folitary tower
Difport loofe fhadows at the midnight hour :
Whence flows the charm thefe hallowed fcenes
  impart,
To warm the fancy, and affect the heart ?
Why fwells the breaft, alive at every pore,
With throbs unknown, and pains unfelt before ?
Why turns the reftlefs glance on every fide
In grateful gloom, or melancholy pride ?
Touched by quick SYMPATHY's myfterious fpring,
Thought's airy fprites in mazy circles wing,
On the fine nerves imprefs a trembling thrill,
And move obedient to the wakeful will,
Till memory's trains in fwift fucceffion rife,
And round RETIREMENT blend harmonic dyes."

There are many readers of poetry who, if the verfes

be well tuned, and the expreffions glowing, pay no regard whatever to the general fcope of the poem ; if they can underftand a fentence, or half a fentence, here and there, they deem this as much as is commonly neceffary in order to relifh the beauties of verfe. For perfons who thus enjoy the harmony of numbers, it may be queftioned whether a more exquifite morfel than this which I have felected could be chofen from the whole compafs of Englifh poetry. We have here "Autumn's dewy ray"; "The breeze with whifpering murmur flowing to *hymn its dirge*"; "Moonlight fparkling on the dimpled main"; and other poetic ornaments in profufion ; and all running into each other with the greateft harmony of verfification. But there are fome who pretend to a tafte for poetry, who have heard that no compofition, whether profe or verfe, can be good which is devoid of meaning; thefe perfons, though they judge, very frequently, in the fame manner with thofe mentioned before, would be much offended if they were fufpected of not comprehending what they admire. To fuch admirers of "The Power of Solitude" the following remarks upon the paffage here quoted are addreffed.

The Poet begins by afking fome queftions, to which he prudently gives an anfwer himfelf; for I am certain it would have puzzled Apollo and the nine Mufes to have hit upon an anfwer refembling it. He

demands why, when autumn's dewy ray sheds the
mild luftre of retiring day ; when awful filence holds
her fullen reign ; when loofe fhadows difport at the
midnight hour ; why, when thefe fcenes are prefent,
the breaft swells alive at every pore, with throbs unknown, and pains unfelt before? The answer is,

" Touched by quick SYMPATHY's myfterious fpring,
Thought's airy fprites in mazy circles wing,
On the fine nerves imprefs a trembling thrill,"

In other words, it is fympathy which caufes thought's airy fprites to fly in mazy circles, and to imprefs the nerves
with a trembling thrill. Now let us afk in turn, with
what thefe fprites of thought fympathize? There muft
either be fomething which the poet has not revealed
with which they fympathize ; or it muft be with fome
of the objects or fcenes which are defcribed as warm-
ing the fancy and fwelling the breaft. That is, the
fprites of thought fympathize with a " dewy ray," or
a " whifpering murmur," or with " moonlight fparkling on the dimpled ftream ;" a rational mind fympa-
thizes with the appearances of inanimate nature. This
fympathy muft indeed be produced by a " myfterious
fpring," which I believe the penetration of no mortal,
before our poet, ever difcovered. But thefe thoughts
after being fet in motion by fympathy,—" move obedient to the wakeful will ;" fympathy, therefore, has
no more to do than to give the firft fpring to thefe

thoughts, and then they are left to the control of the will. The thoughts of the human mind are not very obedient to the will at any time, as the generality of mankind can with forrow teſtify; it is certainly ſtrange then that the thoughts of a perſon in ſuch a ſit-uation as our poet deſcribes can be obedient to his will, while the breaſt is ſwelling, and alive at every pore, with throbs unknown and pains unfelt before. This ſcene of mental diſorder continues,

" 'Till memory's trains in ſwift ſucceſſion riſe,
And round RETIREMENT blend harmonic dyes."

It would ſeem from theſe two laſt lines, that our au-thor does not conſider the trains of memory as belong-ing to the airy and giddy ſprites of thought; ſince they blend their dyes round retirement in ſo harmoni-ous and orderly a manner. This remark, however, may be hypercritical.

The meaning which our author intended to convey was probably this; at the preſence of ſuch ſcenes as are deſcribed in the beginning of the poem, the heart is moved with unuſual ſenſations; confuſed ideas ariſe, which agitate the mind; and laſtly the ſurrounding objects call to remembrance ſome former circumſtan-ces connected with them, upon which the mind repo-ſes in placid reflection. The obſcurity of a paſſage may ariſe from the very nature of its ſubject, or from the length and involution of its periods; both which caufes of obfcurity fhould in poetry be avoided as much as poffible; but if a paffage, whether the expreffions be underftood in their literal acceptation, or in the utmoft latitude which figurative language will permit, be utterly inexplicable by any other method than conjecture, it certainly does not deferve the name of poetry; unlefs, as fome people imagine, fenfe is not a neceffary ingredient in the compofitions of a poet. As the chief object in reviewing the above quotation was to point out its obfcurity, many inferior criticifms have been neglected. We ought not however to pafs over without animadverfion the crouds of epithets; the affected expreffions, fuch as "To hymn its dirge", the reftlefs glance which turns on every fide "with melancholy pride," and others; and the licentious exuberance of ornament with which the paffage upon which we have been commenting, and all the remainder of the poem abound. But thefe are the beauties which charm the prevailing tafte, and without which a new production is in great hazard of meeting with public difapprobation or neglect. The above paffage has been chofen as the fubject of remark, becaufe upon it the author appears to have beftowed the utmoft efforts of his genius. I will clofe thefe obfervations upon the "Power of Solitude," by requefting, that fome one of thofe who admire and underftand this poem, will gratify the lefs difcerning part of the com-

munity, with an explanation of the fubjoined "Invocation to the Spirits of the lighter Gothic Mythology."

"Aërial Elves, who fondly hovering round,
On filver fandals print hiftoric ground,
Who oft with witching mufic charmed his ears,
Danced in his fmiles, and ambufhed in his tears,
As grief or joy their tints alternate fpread,
In floating vifions round your Darwin's head:
Aërial Elves, at Oberon's golden lance,
Who form in myftic ring the fairy dance,
Or, carried on meteors, thro the mazy night
In frolic circles wheel your amorous flight,
O'er the foft lips of artlefs beauty creep,
And paint ftrange fancies on the lover's fleep;
Wind fweet your bugle horns, and fwiftly call
Memory's wild fpirits from the wizard's hall,
Bid them the fcenes of ancient worth reftore,
Chant glory's deathlefs deeds in epic lore,
With fportive fingers trill the harp of time,
And wake reflection by their powers fublime,
Till raptured wifdom hear the facred lay,
And own meek SOLITUDE's impreffive fway."

But light fugitive poems are those which at present
engage the generality of readers. From the multi-
tude of these insect products of genius with which
our preffes swarm, I will select one which I believe
has excited more admiration than most of the ephem-

eral tribe. It was introduced to the public in Philadelphia, accompanied with the following encomiums; " The very elegant verses of " Lodinus " to the fair " invalid, diſplay the moſt ſoothing tenderneſs, and ma- " ny a poetical beauty. They are entitled to the atten- " tion not only of the lady, who is ſo highly greeted, " but of men of taſte and ſenſibility." Theſe verſes were reprinted in New-York, and their praiſes public- ly re-echoed. The following are the verſes alluded to.

" On a beautiful young lady, whoſe health was impaired by the ague and fever.

> " Dark miniſter of many woes !
> That lov'ſt the ſad viciſſitude of pain,
> Now ſhiv'ring mid antarctic ſnows,
> Now a faint pilgrim on Medina's plain—
> Say can no form, leſs fair, thy view engage ?
> Muſt feeble lovelineſs exhauſt thy rage ?
> Oh ! mark the falt'ring ſtep the languid eye,
> And all the anguiſh of her burning ſigh.
> See the faintly ſtruggling ſmile ;
> See reſignation's tear, the while !
> So to the axe the martyr bends his form ;
> So bends the lovely lily to the ſtorm.
> Still, though, ſweet maid ! thy yielding bloom decays,
> And faint, the waning tide of rapture ſtrays ;
> Oh may'ſt thou ſcape Grief's more envenom'd ſmart,
> Nor ever know the ague of the heart !

For rifing from the fun bright plain,
The *bended* lily blooms again ;
But ah ! what life imparting power
Can e'er revive the broken flower ?"

LODINUS.

The "dark minister of many woes" is here said to love "the sad viciffitude of pain". To love pain is a contradiction in terms ; for the very effence of pain is to caufe a feeling which is hateful. It may, however, be faid that the word *pain* is here ufed merely in compliance with our notions ; that what we deem painful this minifter of woe thinks agreeable. It muft be a being very different from any which I have ever heard of, whether celeftial or infernal, which can take delight in freezing at one time among the polar snows, and in fainting at another on the scorching plains of Arabia.

But this gloomy being is next represented as falling into a rage with a lovely maiden, whom, it is to be presumed, he met with on his paffage from the frigid to the torrid zone, and as venting his wrath by bringing upon her those very sensations which he himself was wont to think agreeable. What confufion and contradiction of Ideas are here prefented to the mind ! When Milton's youthful fancy conceived the image of bleak winter, killing, by his rough touch, a fair infant, he broke out thus :

" O faireſt flower no ſooner blown but blaſted,
Soft ſilken primroſe fading timeleſly,
Summer's chief honor, if thou hadſt out-laſted
Bleak winter's force that made thy bloſſom dry ;
For he being amorous on that lovely dye
   That did thy cheek envermeil, thought to kiſs,
But kill'd, alas, and then bewail'd his fatal bliſs."
But to proceed ;

   " See the faintly ſtruggling ſmile ;
   See reſignation's tear, the while !"

When a young lady, to quiet the apprehenſions of thoſe around her, forces a ſmile through her anguiſh, the ſmile may be ſaid to *ſtruggle ;* but, if the rhyme had permitted, this ſmile would have been an emblem of reſignation, much more apt than a tear ; for though a tear may accompany reſignation, it always flows from that anguiſh to which the reſigned temper ſubmits.

   " Still though, ſweet maid ! thy yielding bloom
      decays,
And faint, the waning tide of rapture ſtrays ;"

By " tide of rapture" muſt here be meant the blood. We here ſee a *tide* which is *faint*, and *waning*, and which *ſtrays*, three unuſual attributes of a tide.

   " Oh ! may'ſt thou 'ſcape grief's more envenom'd
      ſmart,
Nor ever know the ague of the heart !"

This " ague of the heart," by what follows, muſt be a diſorder by which the heart is apt to be broken ;

> " For, riſing from the ſun-bright plain,
> The *bended* lily blooms again ;
> But ah ! what life-imparting power
> Can 'eer revive the *broken* flower ?"

It is common to hear of warm hearts, and of cold hearts ; and we have heard of hearts burſt with an-guiſh ; but, I believe, it was never before diſcovered that a heart might periſh in a fit of the ague ; on the contrary, it is uſually ſuppoſed that theſe cold hearts are leaſt liable to ſuffer violence.

Such are the productions which are held up for ad-miration ; in which ſcarcely a ſentence can be found which does not contain an abſurdity. But " antarctic ſnows," and " burning ſighs," and " ſtruggling ſmiles," and " tides of rapture," and " ſun-bright plains," and " life-imparting powers," are charms too powerful to permit an ordinary reader to perceive the greateſt defects. The metaphyſical poets, as they are called, who flouriſhed in England at the beginning of the ſeventeenth century, continually violated the dictates of nature, and neglected the harmony of their verſification, in the eagerneſs of their ſearch after ſtrange turns of thought, and ſubtle diſtinctions. Theſe writers, though they could not claim the merit of ſoothing the ear, of pleaſing the imagination,

or of affecting the heart, at least exercised the under-
standing.   But the fashionable rhymers of the present
day in America, seem to bestow no thought upon
any thing besides the mere dress of their verses ; if
they can procure from the wardrobe of poesy a suffi-
cient supply of dazzling ornaments, wherewith to
deck their intellectual offspring, they are utterly re-
gardless whether the body of sense which these deco-
rations are properly designed to render attractive, be
worthy of attention ; or whether it be mean and dis-
torted, and in danger of being overwhelmed by the
profusion of its ornaments.   There are fashionable
verses of another kind which deserve notice, for faults
of greater importance than foppery of decoration, or
want of meaning.   The verses of this species allure,
not by the gaudiness, but by the lasciviousness of their
dress.   To the admirers and imitators of Moore, the
Translator of Anacreon, who treat so contemptuously
all who presume to censure their indelicacy, I would
recommend the following passage from an ingenious
writer, on the rise and progress of poetry.*   " To
return, therefore, to the decaying state of the poetic
and musical arts in ancient Rome :—As manners and
principles grew more profligate, along with the inor-
dinate growing power and luxury of the empire ; so

* *Dr. Brown.*

the genius of the *poetic* and *mufical* arts kept pace with them.   We hear little of their being applied to the *education* of *youth*, in any period of ancient Rome. On the contrary ; *poem*, which in the days of ancient Greece had been the *handmaid* of *virtue*, was now declared to be the *bawd* of *licentioufnefs ;* and to write immodeft verfes was held a *blamelefs* practice. Thus the art funk fo low, that the name of poet was held unworthy a man of *age* or *dignity.*"

But, after all, it may be faid, why think fo ferioufly of the influence which nonfenfical and immodeft verfes may have upon the community, while there are already fubjects of cenfure fo much more important, and fo much farther extended than any which can ever be produced by a depraved tafte in poetry ?   I might offer an abftrufe argument to prove the advantages which would perhaps refult from the prevalence of a tafte too pure to bear poetry, which tends, not to moral, but merely to intellectual depravity.   It might be faid, that as fome logicians imagine all truths capable of being deduced by a circuitous operation from any one truth, fo the mind by acquiring any one virtue, be it merely a rational excellence, becomes better fitted to receive all other virtues.   There is however too much fubtility in fuch reafoning, where practical inferences are to be deduced.   With regard to the moral impurity of the verfes in queftion, their immediate as well as their remote effects being injurious, and the fmalleft evil being capable of becoming great in extent at leaft, it is manifeft that thefe verfes are not unworthy of animadverfion.

But to fpeak lefs abftractly, it is certainly as reafonable for thofe who feel an intereft in literature, to be defirous of the mental improvement of their countrymen, as it is for the politician to be proud of the conftitution of this country, and for the merchant to exult in her extenfive commerce. And while we are making advances towards perfection in all exterior accomplifhments, and encouraging a tafte for the fine arts; we fhould be careful not to incur the imputation of cultivating thefe external graces at the expenfe of that care which would have been more profitably beftowed upon the improvement of our intellectual powers.

Another reafon which fhould induce every true lover of poetry to oppofe the prevailing corruption of tafte, which, from what I can learn, is continually encreafing, is the contempt which fuch productions as thofe under confideration, eventually excite in the minds of men for the whole race of poets.

In the early ages of fociety, the characters of poet and mufician were united; and the bard enjoyed honors nearly as great as thofe conferred on the fupreme magiftrate. In procefs of time, the poet and the mufician became feparate characters. The mufician was

at firſt both compoſer and performer ; theſe two characters were at length likewiſe ſeparated.   The per-
formers are finally diſtinguiſhed into general perform-
ers who can execute all kinds of muſic, and mere fiddlers, as they are termed, who ſerve to animate and
regulate the motions of dancers.   And it is remarka-
ble that the contempt which is beſtowed upon this
loweſt order of muſicians, is very frequently extended
to all the ſons of harmony ; it is very uſual to hear
them all deſignated by the general appellation of
fiddlers.   The poet's fate, though not ſo hard, is
ſomewhat ſimilar to that of the muſician ; and he has
deſcended from his original height of honor in a like
gradual manner.   The ancient poet comprehended
within the province of his art all ſubjects, however
awful or however minute, in which the welfare of
man is concerned.   In ſucceeding ages, the different
kinds of poetry became diſtinct ſubjects of attention ;
and while ſome continued to blend inſtruction and
pleaſure together ; others, at length, contented them-
ſelves with merely dazzling the imagination and ſoothing the ear.   The final degradation of poetry is due
to thoſe who neglected every conſideration but the
ſound of their productions ; or who heightened by
the charms of language thoſe ideas which are dangerous to innocence.   The whole race of poets have
not eſcaped the reproaches which this laſt order (for I

rank the nonfenfical and the immodeft together) have brought upon themfelves. "I hate *bainting* and *boetry* "too! neither the one nor the other ever did any good," faid George the fecond, when he was informed that Hogarth was about to dedicate to him his celebrated march of the guards to Finchley. Thus a poet is now confidered as one of the ufelefs ornaments of fociety ; a poet, whofe proper and original employment was to render mankind more happy, by exalting their nature. And that the poet might be capable of attaining this noble object, what were the qualifications which it was neceffary for him to poffefs ? It was incumbent upon him to have an ardent love for virtue, that he might defcribe her, not merely with elegance, but with feeling ; a vigorous imagination ; a comprehenfive and difcriminating mind ; extenfive knowledge, keennefs of fenfibility, and powers of language.

Every admirer of genuine poetry fhould be anxious to fee preferved all the remains of her ancient dignity. No production which affumes the guife of poetry, ought to be tolerated, if it poffefs no other recommendation than the glow of its expreffions and tinkling of its fyllables, or the wanton allurement of the ideas which it conveys. It fhould be fcrupuloufly required, that whenever words are put together, they be affembled for fome rational purpofe ; that if the affections be addreffed, the feeling intended to be excited be one of which human nature is fufceptible ; that if an image be prefented to the imagination, its form be diftinguifhable ; and that if reafon be called upon, fomething be expreffed which the mind can comprehend.

THE THIRD SATIRE

OF

JUVENAL.

ARGUMENT.

Umbritius, an Arufpex, and a friend of our author, difgufted at the prevalence of vice, and the total difregard of needy and unaffuming virtue, is introduced on the point of quitting Rome. The poet accompanies him fome little way from the city, when the honeft exile, no longer able to fupprefs his indignation, ftops fhort, and in a ftrain of animated invective, acquaints him with the caufes of his retirement.

This fatire is managed with wonderful ingenuity, the way by which Juvenal conducts his friend out of the city, is calculated to raife a thoufand tender images in his mind; and when after lingering a moment at the gate, Umbritius ftops to look at it for the laft time, in a fpot endeared by religion, covered with the venerable relics of antiquity, and in itfelf eminently beautiful; we are tempted to liften with uncommon attention to the farewell of the folitary fugitive.

ARGUMENT.

What he fays may be arranged under the following heads, that flattery and vice are the only thriving arts at Rome ; that in thefe, particularly the firft, foreigners have a manifeft fuperiority over the natives, and confequently engrofs all favor ; that the poor are univerfally expofed to fcorn and infult ; that the general habits of extravagance render it difficult for them to fubfift, and that a crowded capital fubjects them to numberlefs inconveniences unknown in the country (on the tranquility and fecurity of which he feelingly dictates) ; he then adverts again to the peculiar fufferings of the poorer citizens, from the want of a well regulated police ; thefe he illuftrates by a variety of examples, and concludes in a ftrain of pathos and beauty, which winds up the whole with fingular effect.

Gifford.

D. J. JUVENALIS

SATYRA III. v. 1—8.

QUAMVIS digreffu veteris confufus amici,

Laudo tamen vacuis quod fedem figere Cumis

Deftinet, atque unum civem donare Sibyllæ.

Janua Baiarum eft, et gratum littus, amæni

Seceffus : ego vel Prochytam præpono Saburræ.

Nam quid tam miferum, et tam folum vidimus, ut non

Deterius credas horrere incendia, lapfus

Tectorum affiduos, ac mille pericula fævæ

THE THIRD SATIRE
OF JUVENAL. v. 1—12.

THO' griev'd to lofe my firm and ancient friend,

I praife his purpofe and his choice commend,

At lonely Cumæ, fix'd to place his feat,

And with one citizen the Sybil greet. *

To Baiæ Cumæ leads ; her flighted coaft

Of many a fweet and cool recefs can boaft ;

Tho', fooner would I make fome rock my home,

Than dwell amidft the crowds and noife of Rome.

Can gloom or defert more alarm the mind,

Than all the terrors of the town combin'd ?

When flames wide-wafting burft and blaze around,

And houfes, ceafelefs falling, fhake the ground ?

---

* *There was a temple at Cumæ, dedicated to the Sybil.*

Urbis, et Augufto recitanteis menfe poëtas ?

Sed dum tota domus rhedâ componitur unâ,

Subftitit ad veteres arcus, madidamque Capenam,

Hic, ubi nocturnae Numa conftituebat amicae.

Nunc facri fontis nemus, et delubra locantur

Judaeis, quorum cophìnus faenumque fuppellex.

Omnis enim populo mercedem pendere juffa eft

Arbor, et ejectis mendicat fylva Camaenis.

In vallem Egeriae defcendimus, et fpeluncas

Diffimiles veris ; quanto praeftantius effet

Numen aquae, viridi fi margine clauderet undas

Herba, nec ingenuum violarent marmora tophum :

And, while the dog-ftar glows with baleful light,

Where raving poets feize you and recite ?

Now ftopt my friend, when juft without the wall,

To wait the cart that brought his little all,

Where ancient trees diffufe a facred fhade,

And Numa nightly met th' Egerian maid ;

But now a miferable wand'ring train

Poffefs the fount, and confecrated fane ;

And fince the grove is let to fordid hire,

The mufes all indignantly retire.

Next, to Egeria's vale we flow defcend,

And mark the grots which art has ftrove to mend ;

How vain her efforts—fure the nymph would feem

Far, far more prefent, if her gurgling ftream

The frefh and verdant turf confin'd alone,

Nor marble dar'd pollute the native ftone.

Hic tunc Umbricius quando artibus inquit honeftis

Nullus in urbe locus, nulla emolumenta laborum,

Res hodie minor eft herĕ quàm fuit, atque eadem cras

Deteret exiguis aliquid : proponimus illuc

Ire, fatigatas ubi Dædalus exuit alas ;

Dum nova canities, dum prima, et recta fenectus,

Dum fupereft Lachefi quod torqueat, et pedibus me

Porto meis, nullo dextram subeunte bacillo.

Cedamus patriâ : vivant Arturius iftic

Umbritius then (while forrow fwell'd my breaft)

His rage and grief in manly ftrain expreft—

Since then my friend within this city's bound,

No room for honorable arts is found;

Since ftill I labour on without reward,

And none my merits or my toil regard;

Whilft all my pittance gradual melts away,

Tomorrow lefs'ning what remains today;

From vice and Rome I fly to that lone fhore,

Where wearied Dædalus his flight gave o'er.

While age not yet has filver'd o'er my head,

Not yet all traces of my youth are fled;

While health and vigour ftill my veins fupply,

And on no ftaff my fteady fteps rely;

Farewell to Rome—let thofe at Rome remain,

That vile, deceitful, mercenary train

Et Catulus : maneant qui nigrum in candida vertunt,

Queis facile est ædem conducere flumina, portus,

Siccandam eluviem, portandum ad busta cadaver,

Et prabere caput dominâ venale sub hastâ.

Quondam hi cornicines, et municipalis arenae

Perpetui comites, notaeque per oppida buccae,

Munera nunc edunt, et verso pollice vulgi

Quemlibet occidunt populariter : inde reversi

Conducunt foricas : et cur non omnia ? cùm sint

Quales ex humili magna ad fastigia rerum

Extollit, quoties voluit fortuna, jocari.

Who praife or flander, flatter or attack,

And change the black to white, the white to black,

With equal eafe—Arturius thou remain ;

And ye who bear the dead, the kennels drain,

Farm rivers, ports, build temples, auctions hold,

Fame, honor, confcience, throw away for gold.

Thefe once were trumpeters, and gain'd renown

For ftrength of lungs, thro' ev'ry county town—

But now grown rich, the populace they court

By giving fhews, and murd'ring men for fport ;

From thefe return'd, again their av'rice wakes,

Again the kennel drains, or farms again the jakes.

" *And why not every thing ? fince thefe are they",

Whom fortune vifits with her brighteft ray ;

Are fuch, as in her wild and fportive mood,

She joys to raife above the wife and good.

*Gifford.

Quid Romae faciam? mentiri nefcio: librum

Si malus eft nequeo laudare, et pofcere: motus

Aftrorum ignoro: funus promitere patris

Nec volo, nec poffum: ranarum viscera nunquam

Infpexi: ferre ad nuptam quae mittit adulter,

Quae mandat, nôrunt alii: me nemo miniftro

Fur erit, atque ideò nulli comes exeo, tanquam

Mancus, et extinctae corpus non utile dextrae.

What fhould I do at Rome ? I cannot lie;
Nor laugh with folly, nor with vice comply ;
I cannot, if a book be bad, admire,
And, while I nod, extol the poet's fire ;
I ne'er have learnt the virtues of the toad ; ·
Nor know I what the rolling ftars forbode ;
Tho' others may, I neither can nor will
Predict a father's death, nor boaft the fkill,
Th' adult'rers notes or prefents to convey,
"* And bribe a matron's innocence away."
(And tho' the world may deem my fcruples vain,)
No thief thro' me flagitious wealth fhall gain ;
And hence I pafs my life in friendlefs gloom,
And walk unmark'd the crowded ftreets of Rome ;
But whilft the great my zeal and fervice fcorn,
What virtues, say, the chofen friend adorn,
To whom they dare the fecret foul reveal ?
The holy league, by mutual guilt, they feal ;

" *And bribe a virgin's innocence away".   JOHNSON.

D

Quis nunc diligitur nisi confcius, et cui fervens

Æftuat occultis animus, femperque tacendis ?

Nil tibi fe debere putat, nil conferet unquam,

Participem qui te fecreti fecit honefti.

Carus erit Verri, qui Verrem tempore, quo vult,

Accufare poteft : tanti tibi non fit opaci

Omnis arena Tagi, quodque in mare volvitur aurum,

Ut fomno careas, ponendaque præmia fumas

Triftis, et à magno femper timearis amico,

Quœ nunc divitibus gens acceptiffima noftris,

Et quos praecipuè fugiam, properabo fateri,

Nec pudor obftabit.   Non poffum ferre Quirites,

He fhares the heart, in thefe polluted times,

Whofe confcience pants, with fecret, namelefs, crimes.

He owes you nothing, nor will e'er beftow

Who trufts a fecret 'tis no crime to know.

Him, who arraigns, when Verres felf thinks fit,

Will grateful Verres to his heart admit.

Not all the gold, that refts on Tagus' fhores,

Not all the gold, his ftream in Ocean pours,

Should tempt thee to forego thy nightly reft,

(That boon unvalued of the guiltlefs breaft)

And, whilft thy patron fears thee, truft thy fate

To that feign'd love, which foon muft change to hate.

Mark now the wretches by the rich careft,

And whom, I freely own, I chief deteft ;

I cannot bear (ye nobles fpare the frown)

Rome chang'd and funk into a Grecian town ;

Græcam urbem, quamvis quota portio facis Achææ ?
Jam pridem Syrus in Tiberim defluxit Orontes,
Et linguam, et mores et cum tibicine chordas
Obliquas, nec non gentilia tympana fecum
Vexit, et ad Circum juffas proftare puellas.
Ite, quibus grata eft picta lupa barbara mitra.
Rufticus ille tuus fumit trechedipna, Quirine,
Et ceromatico fert niceteria collo.
Hic altâ Sicyonê, aft hic Amydonê relictâ,
Hic Andrô, ille Samo, hic Trallibus, aut Alabandis.
Efquilias, dictumque petunt a vimine collem,
Vifcera magnarum domuum, dominique futuri.
Ingenium velox, audacia perdita, fermo
Promptus, et Ifaeo torrentior : ede quid illum

Yet fmall the portion is by Greece fupplied :

Orontes pours his vaft and black'ning tide,

And whelms the Tiber, with his foreign waves :

His language, manners, minftrels, ftrumpets, flaves

He bears along.   O Romulus behold ;

See foreign robes thy ruftic now infold ;

See ! on his naked neck, which oil befmears

The Circus prize, he now exulting wears.

From every Grecian town and Grecian fhore

In countlefs fwarms, the famifh'd natives pour ;

Rome, Rome, is fought by all the mingled band,

Who thick as locufts overfpread the land ;

Quick into palaces they work their way,

The minions firft, where foon as lords they fway,

Prompt, fluent, artful, treacherous and bold,

* No dangers daunt them and no ties can hold.

---

* *No dangers daunt him, and no labors tire.*
                    JOHNSON's Van. of Hu. wifhes.

Effe putes ? quemvis hominem fecum attulit ad nos;
Grammaticus, rhetor, geometres, pictor, aliptes,
Augur, fchaenobates, medicus, magus ; omnia novit :
Græculus efuriens, in cælum, jufferis, ibit.
Ad fummam, non Maurus erat, nec Sarmata, nec Thrax,
Qui fumpfit pennas, mediis fed natus Athenis.
Horum ego non fugiam conchilia ? me prior ille
Signabit, fultus thoro meliore recumbet,
Advectus Romam, quo pruna et coctona, vento ?
Ufque adeo nihil eft, quod noftra infantia cælum

You fee this Greek ; fpeak, what fhall he become ?

Whoe'er you pleafe, is brought in him to Rome ;

Grammarian, Rhetor, Painter or Phyfician,

Carver, Cook, Aftronomer, Magician,

Hunger all arts and fciences beftows,

" *And bid him go to heav'n, to heav'n he goes !"

Nor Moor, nor Gaul, nor Thracian was the wight,

Who thro' the fkies purfued his daring flight.

A Greek he was, in midft of Athens born.

What fhall I bear their ftate ? my honeft fcorn

Muft I fubdue ? fhall they who hither came

With prunes and rotten figs, now boaft their claim.

To fign before me ; at the feftive board

U furp the couch that's neareft to the lord ?

And is it nothing, that my infant eye

Firft ope'd its lids upon a Roman fky ?

---

* *Dryden.*

Hausit Aventini, baccâ nutrita Sabinâ ?
Quid, quod adulandi gens prudentiffima laudat
Sermonem indocti, faciem deformis amici,
Et longum invalidî collum cervicibus æquat
Herculis, Antæum procul à tellure tenentis ?
Miratur vocem auguftam, quâ deterius nec
Ille fonat, quo mordetur gallina marito.
Hæc eadem licet et nobis laudare : fed illis
Creditur : an melior cum Thaida fuftinet, aut cum
Uxorem comædus agit, vel Dorida nullo
Cultam palliolo ? mulier nempe ipfa videtur,
Non perfona loqui : vacua et plana omnia dicas
Infra ventriculum, et tenui diftantia rimâ.

And nothing, that beneath the Sabine ſhade,

My childhood flouriſh'd and exulting play'd ?

Profoundly ſkill'd in flattery's potent art,

By well turn'd praiſe, they gain and keep the heart :

Extol the learning of the unlearn'd friend ;

The beauties of the gorgon face commend ;

The narrow neck and cheſt, unbluſhing dare,

To all the ſtrength of Hercules compare ;

And at the ſqueaking voice enraptur'd ſeem,

Whoſe piercing tones ſurpaſs the peacock's ſcream.

We too can flatter : True ; but who believes ?

What fool ſo ſtupid, that our praiſe deceives ?

Whilſt they, with eaſe, aſſume each various part,

And, all they ſay, ſeems inſtant from the heart.

The wife, the miſtreſs or the undreſs'd fair, ⎫
Behold they perſonate ; deceiv'd you ſwear ⎬
No actor, but the woman's ſelf is there. ⎭

Nec tamen Antiochus, nec erit mirabilis illic
Aut Stratocles, aut cum molli Demetrius Hæmo.
Natio comœda eſt : rides ? majore cachinno
Concutitur : flet, ſi lacrymas adſpexit amici.
Nec dolet : igniculum brumæ ſi tempore poſcas,
Accipit endromidem : ſi dixeris, æſtuo, ſudat.
Non ſumus ergo pares : melior qui ſemper et omni
Nocte dieque poteſt alienum ſumere vultum ;
A facie jactare manus, laudare paratus,
Si bene ructavit ſi rectum minxit amicus :
Si trulla inverſo crepitum dedit aurea fundo.
Præterea ſanctum nihil eſt, et ab inguine tutum :
Non matrona Laris, non filia virgo, neque ipſe
Sponſus levis adhuc, non filius antē pudicus.

Yet here no mimes of note your wonder raife,

And not a Greek but equal art difplays.

The patron laughs——a louder laugh replies :

He weeps——a torrent rufhes from their eyes :

Complains of heat——they fweat——demands a fire,

They fhiver, and their fhaggy cloaks require.

We quit the field : fuperior thefe we own,

Whofe hearts can never, by the face, be known,

Which fhifts at will, its well affum'd difguife,

And ftill to fuit another's vifage, lies.

With thefe, we own, t'were madnefs to contend,

Who praife the coughing, or the belching friend,

At Folly's whims, their hands applauding raife,

Or on the freaks of Vice, with tranfport gaze.

Add, none are fafe from their infatiate luft,

Nor wife, nor fon, nor daughter can you truft ;

Horum fi nihil eft, aviam refupinat amici.

Scire volunt fecreta domus, atque inde timeri.

Et quoniam cœpit Græcorum mentio, tranfi

Gymnafia, atque audi facinus majoris abollæ.

Stoicus occidit Baream, delator amicum,

Difcipulumque fenex, ripâ nutritus in illâ,

Ad quam Gorgonei delapfa eft pinna caballi.

Non eft Romano cuiquam locus hic, ubi regnat

Protogenes aliquis, vel Diphilus, aut Erimanthus :

Qui gentis vitio nunquam partitur amicum,

Solus habet : nam, cum facilem ftillavit in aurem

Exiguum de naturæ patriæque veneno,

None, none are facred ; and if these fhould lack,

Your grandame's felf undaunted they attack—

Your fecrets next, with filent art, explore,

And foon are fear'd, altho' defpifed before.

And fince of Greeks we fpeak; next view their fchools;

Thence virtue iffues arm'd with all her rules—

Yon Stoic mark, in coarfeft garb array'd ;

His deareft friend that hoary wretch betray'd

And flew—a Greek, tranfported from that fhore,

When the wing'd hack a pinion dropt of yore—

No place for Romans here, where Grecians fway,

And drive the Patron's ancient friends away ;

And bear no rivals near their jealous throne,

But claim and govern all the friend alone.

Their pois'nous hints into his ear they pour,

And lo, I'm fpurn'd with infult from the door ;

E

Limine fummoveor : perierunt tempora longi

Servitii : nufquam minor eft jactura clientis.

Quod porro officium (ne nobis blandiar) aut quod

Pauperis hic meritum : fi curet nocte togatus

Currere, cum praetor lictorem impellat, et ire

Praecipitem jubeat dudum vigilantibus orbis,

Ne prior Albinam, aut Modiam, collega falutet ?

Divitis hic fervi cludit latus ingenuorum

Filius : alter enim, quantum in legione tribuni

Accipiunt, donat Calvinae, vel Catienae,

Ut femel atque iterum fuper illam palpitet : at tu,

My tedious flav'ry left without reward,

Since none a clients trifling lofs regard.

Trifling indeed ; for why the truth deny ?

What merits have we that we rate fo high ?

Scarce rous'd, you feize your cloak before the dawn,

But find your patron is already gone.

Long fince awake, the childlefs matrons wait

The venal tribe, who crowd their early ftate.

The prætor hurries on, in anxious fpeed,

And bids his guards with brifker pace proceed :

Hafte left my colleague gain the firft falute ;

And they my flownefs to neglect impute—

Mark the rich flave with nobles in his train ;

Why they fo humble, or why he fo vain ?

The lavifh flave, undoubting, throws away

For one embrace, a tribune's ample pay :

Cum tibi veftiti facies fcorti placet, hæres,

Et dubitas altâ Chionem deducere fellâ

Da teftem Romæ tam fanctum, quam fuit hofpes

Numinis Idæi : procedat vel Numa, vel qui

Servavit trepidam flagranti ex æde Minervam :

Protinus ad cenfum, de moribus ultima fiet

Quæftio : quot pafcit fervos, quot poffidet agri

Jugera, quam multâ magnaque paropfide cœnat.

Quantum quifque fuâ nummorum fervat in arcâ,

Tantum habet et fidei.   Jures licet et Samothracum,

Et noftrorum aras ; contemnere fulmina pauper

Creditur atque deos, dis ignofcentibus ipfis.

Whilſt they, confounded by the price, retreat ;

Nor dare to hand the wanton from her ſeat—

Pure in his thoughts, unblemiſh'd in his life,

Your witneſs comes—his voice muſt end the ſtrife ;

Nor Numa's ſelf more holy, not the hoſt

Of Cybele could brighter virtue boaſt ;

Nor he who ruſh'd intrepid through the fire,

And ſav'd Minerva's ſelf ; what more require ?

What's his eſtate, the judges firſt demand ;

Say, what his ſlaves, his equipage, his land ?

If rich, believe him ; but if poor, he lies ;

The wrath of heav'n, we know, the poor deſpiſe.

What tho' he dare the angry bolts of Jove,

And all the gods atteſt, his words to prove ?

Heed, heed him not, they cry, the wretch muſt live,

And e'en the gods his perjuries forgive—

Quid, quod materiam præbet caufasque jocorum
Omnibus hic idem ? fi fœda ac fciffa lacerna,
Si toga fordidula, et ruptâ calceus alter
Pelle patet : vel fi, confuto vulnere, craffum
Atque receus linum oftendit non una cicatrix.
Nil habit infelix paupertas durius in fe,
Quam quod ridiculos homines facit.   Exe∴t, inquit,
Si pudor eft, et de pulvino furgat equeftri,
Cujus res legi non fufficit, et fedeant hic
Lenonum pueri quocunque in fornice natī.
Hic plaudat nitidi præconis filius, inter

Add, that the poor continual taunts provoke;

No fool fo dull, but points at them his joke.

If foil'd the garment, or if fomewhat worn,

Or aukward patches fhow where lately torn,

Or thro' the op'ning fhoe the foot appear,

They gather round, and circulate the fneer.

O poverty! of all thy num'rous ills,

This chief the foul with bitter anguifh fills;

Contempt muft ftill, with ftruggling heart, be borne,

And laughing fools, with fafety, fhow their fcorn.

Quit, quit thofe benches, angry Lectius cries,

Thofe benches are the Knights', nay, quick arife.

'Tis well, I yield, with rev'rence, I retreat,

That pander's fons may hold the vacant feat,

No matter from what ftews firft fpawn'd abroad;

Here let the wealthy crier's heir applaud.

Pinnirapi cultos juvenes, juvenefque laniftæ

Sic libitum vano, qui nos diftinxit, Othoni.

Quis gener hic placuit cenfu minor, atque puellæ

Sarcinulis impar ? quis pauper fcribitur hæres ?

Quando in concilio eft ædilibus ? agmine facto

Debuerant olim tenues migraffe Quirites.

Haud facile emergunt, quorum virtutibus obftat

Res angufta domi. Sed Romæ durior illis

Let fencers here, and effenc'd beaux be plac'd ;

Fit arbiters to rule the public tafte !

'Tis thus vain Otho's pleafure is obey'd,

Whofe wifdom firft, the juft diftinction made—

Who e'er his daughter to a poor man gave,

Tho' wife, accomplifh'd, honeft, learn'd, and brave ?

When were the poor e'er mention'd in a will,

Or call'd to aid the Ædile with their fkill ?

Long fince, fhonld they have fought fome diftant fhore,

And borne thefe infults and this fcorn no more.

*Throughout the world the mournful truth's confeft ;

Virtue, by poverty's thick gloom oppreft,

Hardly breaks forth into her native day ;

But here, more darkling still, fhe gropes her way.

Life's neceffary means here all are high,

The ftricteft care will fcarce the charge fupply.

---

*The mournfnl truth is every where confeft.
JOHNSON.

Conatus : magno hofpitium miferabile ; magno
Servorum ventres ; et frugi coenula magno.
Fictilibus coenare pudet, quod turpe negarît
Tranflatus fubito ad Marfos menfamque Sabellam,
Contentufque illic Veneto duroque cucullo.
Pars magna Italiæ eft, fi verum admittimus, in quâ
Nemo togam fumit, nifi mortuus : ipfa dierum
Feftorum herbofo colitur fi quando theatro
Majeftas, tandemque redit ad pulpita notum
Exodium, cum perfonæ pallentis hiatum
In gremio matris formidat rufticus infans ;
Æquales habitus illic, fimilefque videbis
Orcheftram et populum : clari velamen honoris,

A frugal fupper, wretched lodgings hire,

And fervants' board, enormous fums require.

Here earthen-ware we fcorn, but change the place,

And at the Sabine board, 'tis no difgrace ;

What e'er the difh, we relifh well the fare,

And coarfeft hoods, without a fcruple, wear.

Great part of Italy (the truth confefs)

Gives only to the dead the Roman drefs,

The fplendid gown—nay e'en on feftal days,

When theatres of turf again they raife ;

When the known farce again the ruftics choofe,

That ftill their laughter, and loud mirth renews ;

While clings the infant to his mother's fide,

Scar'd at the mafk that opes the mouth fo wide ;

E'en then both rich and poor are cloth'd alike ;

Save that, the crowd with proper awe to ftrike,

Sufficiunt tunicæ fummis ædilibus albæ.

Hic ultra vires habitus nitor ; hîc aliquid plus,

  Quam fatis eft : interdum alienâ fumitur arcâ.

Commune id vitium eft : hic vivimus ambitiofâ

Paupertate omnes : quid te moror ? Omnia Romæ

Cum pretio : quid das, ut Coffum aliquando falutes ?

Ut te refpiciat claufo Veiento labello ?

Ille metit barbam, crinem hic deponit amati :

Plena domus libis venalibus : accipe, et iftud

Fermentum tibi habe : præftare tributa clientes

  Cogimur, et cultis augere peculia fervis.

And prove their rank, the Ædiles dref in white.

But here one glare of fplendor meets the fight ;

Splendor that few fupport ; but if opprefſt,

We plunge our hands into a neighbors cheſt.

This, this, the common vice we juſtly call,

Ambitious poverty deſtroys us all.

But why detain you ? All at Rome is bought,

And all we feek, muſt with a bribe be fought.

A paſſing nod fhall haughty Coſſus deign ?

Produce the bribe, or not a fmile you gain ;

The blackeſt crimes Veiento dares impute,

But fhew the bribe, and lo, the wretch is mute,

This minion fhaves his beard, this lops his hair,

The clients run, and all their prefents bear.

'Tis thus the fav'rite fwells his growing ſtore

Receiving ſtill, and aſking ſtill for more—

F.

Quis timet, aut timuit gelida Praenefte ruinam,

Aut pofitis nemorofa inter juga Volfiniis, aut

Simplicibus Gabiis, aut proni Tiburis arce ?

Nos urbem colimus tenui tibicine fultam

Magna parte fui : nam fic labentibus obftat

Vilicus, et veteris rimae contexit hiatum ;

Securos pendente jubet dormire ruinâ

Vivendum eft illic, ubi nulla incendia, nulli

For fince thefe flaves alone, the patron fway,

This is a tax we all are forc'd to pay.

Left fome old building by a fudden fall

Should crufh his frame, beneath the pond'rous wall,

What peafant fears at Tiber's lofty feat,

At Gabii or Prænefte's cool retreat?

But 'midft continual dread, we ftill remain,

Where feeble props the trembling vaults fuftain.

For thus, fo wife, fo provident their care,

The finking walls our mafter-ftewards repair;

Then bid us reft and all our terrors end,

Whilft death and ruin o'er our heads impend.

Quick, let us feek, my friend fome quiet fhade,

Where no rude fears the midnight couch invade.

No terrors hover round the throbbing head,

And drive you trembling from a reftlefs bed;

Nocte metus. Jam poſcit aquam, jam frivola transfert,

Ucalegon : tabulata tibi jam tertia fumant :

Tu neſcis : nam ſi gradibus trepidatur ab imis,

Ultimus ardebit, quem tegula ſola tuetur

A pluviâ, molles ubi reddunt ova columbæ.

Lectus erat Codro Proculâ minor, utceoli ſex,

Ornamentum abacî ; nec non et parvulus infra

Cantharus, et recubans ſub eodem marmore Chiron ;

Jamque vetus Græcos ſervabat ciſta libellos,

Et divina opici rodebant carmina mures.

Nil habuit Codrus : quis enim negat ? et tamen illud

Perdidit infelix totum nil : ultimus autem

No fudden flames difpel the gloom of night,

And pour their horrors on th' aftonifh'd sight.

From the next houfe the burfting flames arife,

And mount in blazing volumes to rhe fkies ;

The tenants fly with all their hafte can take——

The floors beneath you fmoke——nor ftill you wake ;

For fince its ravages begin below,

Your garret laft the raging peft will know.

The wretched Codrus own'd but one fhort bed ;

Six little pitchers grac'd the cupboard head ;

Next thefe a jug, for ufe defigned, not fhow ;

A marble Chiron fpread his leangth below ;

In an old cheft the Grecian bards were laid,

Where mice, barbarian-like, fecurely prey'd.

Codrus had nothing ; thus the world would fay :

Yet all that nothing, foon was torn away——

Ærumnæ cumulus, quod nudum et fruftra rogantem
Nemo cibo, nemo hofpitio, tectoque, juvabit.
Si magna Afturici cecidit domus, horrida mater,
Pullati proceres, differt vadimonia prætor :
Tunc gemimus cafus urbis, tunc odimus ignem.
Ardet adhuc, et jam accurrit qui marmora donet,
Conferat impenfas : hic nuda et candida figna ;
Hic aliquid prœclarum Euphranoris et Polycleti ;
Hic Afianorum vetera ornamenta deorum.
Hic libros dabit, et forulas, mediamque Minervam ;
Hic modium argenti : meliora ac plura reponit

And ſtill the wretch's woes are not compleat ;

Cold, hungry, bare, behold he roams the ſtreet,

Whilſt all, the mercy that he aſks, deny,

And none a bed, or clothes, or food ſupply——

But ſhould Aſturius' lofty palace fall ;

Grief ſpreads around, and horror ſeizes all ;

Juſtice is ſtaid, the matron rends her hair,

And Knights and Peers their blackeſt garments wear——

'The chances of the town then all bewail,

Then all at fires with double hatred rail.

Still flames the pile——when lo the flatterers haſte,

And pour their riches to ſupply the waſte ;

A nobler dome, with eager zeal, they raiſe,

One brings materials, one the workmen pays,

Statues, the boaſt of Greece, that dome adorn,

And ornaments, from Aſian temples torn,

In gifts of uſe or luxury they vie,

And book and vaſes, plate and gold ſupply ;

Perficus orborum lautiffimus, et meritò jam

Sufpectus, tanquam ipfe fuas incenderit ædes.

Si potes avelli Ciircenfibus, optima Soræ,

Aut Fabrateriæ, domus, aut Frufinone, paratur.

Quanti nunc tenebras unum conducis in annum !

Hortulus hic, puteufque breuis, nec refte movendus,

In tenues plantas facili diffunditur hauftu.

Vive bidentis amans, et culti villicus horti,

Unde epulum poffis centum dare Pythagoreis.

Thus by his lofs Afturius fwell'd his ftore,

Tho' known as richeft of the rich before.

And all fufpect him author of the fire,

* " That burnt his palace, but to build it higher."

To leave the Circus fports, could'ft thou endure,

In fome neglected burgh thou might'ft procure

A fweet retreat, at fmaller coft, than here

Thou hir'ft a dungeon for a fingle year——

There ftreams gufh forth, fpontaneous, from the ground,

And pour their rills with eafy lapfe around,

And cheer the plants, and frefhen all the green ;

There live enamour'd of the peaceful fcene,

There feize the plough, and learn the ruftic's fkill ;

And there, well pleas'd, thy little garden till ;

Whofe frefh and wholefome herbs, I dare engage,

Shall feaft an hundred like the Samian fage.

---

* *Dryden*

Est aliquid quocunque loco, quocunque receſſu,
Unius ſeſe dominum feciſſe lacertae.
Plurimus hic æger moritur vigilando : ſed illum
Languorem peperit cibus imperfectus et hærens
Ardenti ſtomacho : nam quae meritoria ſomnum
Admittunt ? magnís opibus dormitur ín urbe.
Inde caput morbi : rhedarum tranſitus arcto
Vicorum inflexu et ſtantis convicia mandrae
Eripient ſomnum Druſo vituliſque marinis.
Si vocat officium, turbâ cedente, vehetur
Divès, et ingenti curret ſuper ora Liburno,
Atque obiter leget, aut ſcribet, vel dormiet intus :
Namque facit ſomnum clauſâ lectica fenſtrâ.

However rude and diftant the recefs,

'Tis fomething e'en one lizard to poffefs—

Here rack'd with fumes by indigeftion bred,

The fick man lingers on a reftlefs bed ;

In filent anguifh rolls his fleeplefs eyes,

That ftill glare round, when he exhaufted, dies.

Our rented houfes no repofe allow ;

The balm of fleep the rich alone can know ;

'And this the fource whence fell difeafes flow.

Hark the loud waggons thund'ring thro' the ftreet,

The brawls and curfes when their drivers meet.

Tumult like this the torpid Seal would wake ;

Nay ftupid Drufus from his flumbers fhake.

Behold the rich man to the levee hafte,

By footmen borne, and in a litter plac'd,

Whilft as he moves the fervile crowd gives way ;

He reads or writes ; perchance excludes the day

Ante tamen veniet : nobis properantibus obſtat
Unda prior : magno populus premit agmine lumbos
Qui ſequitur ; ferit hic cubito, ferit aſſere duro
Alter ; at hic tignum capiti incutit, ille metretam :
Pinguia crura luto, planâ mox undique magnâ
Calcor, et in digito clavus mihi militis hæret.
Nonne vides, quanto celebretur ſportula fumo ?
Centum convivæ ; ſequitur ſua quemque culina.
Corbulo vix ferret tot vaſa ingentia, tot res
Impoſitas capiti, quot recto vertice portat
Servulus infelix, et curſu ventilat ignem.

And takes his nap—yet reaches firft the door;

While we, impeded by the crowd before,

And urg'd behind, with painful efforts ftrive,

And bruis'd and torn, beyond the time arrive.

Tho' preft, nay almoft trampled by the throng,

Up to the knees in mud I wade along;

Sharp elbows gore, my head's affail'd with blows

And foldiers' hob-nail'd fhoes indent my toes.

See from the dole, what clouds of fmoke arife;

Each to receive his ftated portion flies;

Each with his flave, an hundred guefts attend.

With head on high, and neck that fears to bend,

Difhes on difhes pil'd the flave muft bear,

(A weight that Corbulo could fcarce uprear,)

Nor bear alone; but run beneath his load,

Left all the dainties cool upon the road.

G

Scinduntur tunicæ sartæ ; modò longa corufcat,

Sarraco veniente, abies, atque altera pinum

Plauftra vehunt, nutant altè, populoque minantur.

Nam fi procubuit, qui faxa Liguftica portat,

Axis, et everfum fudit fuper agmina montem,

Quid fupereft de corporibus ? quis membra, quis offa

Invenit ? obtritum vulgi perit omne cadaver,

More animæ : domus interea fecura patellas

Jam lavat, et buccâ foculum excitat, et fonat unctis

Strigilibus ; et pleno componit lintea gutto.

Hæc inter pueros variè properantur : at ille

Jam fedet in ripâ, tetrumque novitius horret

Opprest beneath the weight of elm or pine,

The pond'rous waggons move in dreadful line,

The beams immenfe with tott'ring motion go,

And threaten death on all who pafs below.

Behold that carriage heap'd with maffy ftones ;

The buildings tremble and the pavement groans ;

Ye Gods ! the axle fails, and all beneath

Are crufh'd, and perifh in promifcuous death—

Not e'en their mangled carcafes remain,

No member, joint, nor atom of the flain.

The body, like the foul, amaz'd you find,

Has fled, nor left a fingle trace behind.

His fellow flaves, meanwhile, exempt from care,

With fruitlefs hafte, their fev'ral tafks prepare ;

While *he poor wretch, abruptly hurried down,

Aw'd by the terrors of grim Charon's frown,

---

* The flave who was carrying the fportula.   Some Commentators fuppofe the mafter to be here intended, and indeed
the obfcurity of the original leaves fufficient room for various conjectures.

Porthmea, nec fperat cœnofi gurgitus alnum
Infelix, nec habet, quem porrigat, ore trientem.
Refpice nunc alia, ac diverfa pericula noctis:
Quod fpatium tectis fublimibus, unde cerebrum
Tefta ferit, quoties rimofa et curta feneftris
Vafa cadunt, · quanto percuffum pondere fignent
Et lædant filicem. Poffis ignavus haberi,
Et fubiti cafus improvidus, ad cœnam fi
Inteftatus eas; adeo tot fata, quot illâ
Nocte patent vigiles, te prætereunte, feneftræ.
Ergo optes, votumque feras miferabile tecum,
Ut fint contentæ patulas effundere pelves.
Ebrius ac petulans, qui nullum fortè cecidit,

Now fits dejected, on the gloomy fhore,

Without a farthing to get ferried o'er.

Nor thefe the only dangers of the night ;

Behold our houfes——what a fearful height,

For pots to fall upon the paffing head.

Now broken jars, in garret windows fpread,

With mighty weight and force, defcending rufh,

Break the firm ftone, and all the pavement crufh.

He's madly thoughtlefs of impending ill,

Who leaves his home before he figns his will ;

Since death in ambufh lies, and marks his prey,

From ev'ry cafement, that o'erlooks the way.

Move flowly on, and breathe a wretched vow

That pans alone may pour their ftreams below.

The drunken bully, ftrives to fleep in vain,

Who feeks his couch, before his man is flain.

Dat pœnas ; noctem patitur lugentis amicum

Pelidæ, cubat in faciem, mox deinde fupinus ;

Ergo non aliter poterit dormire : quibufdam

Somnum rixa facit : fed, quamvis improbus annis,

Atque mero fervens, cavet hunc, quem coccina læna

Vitari jubet, et comitum longiffimus ordo,

Multum præterea flammarum, et aënea lampas.

Me quem luna folet deducere, vel breve lumen

Candelæ, cujus difpenfo et tempero filum,

Feels all the tortures that Pelides knew,

When raging Hector his Patroclus flew ;

When " * now fupine now prone the hero lay,

" And fhifts his fides impatient for the day."

But fhould a brawl his thirft of blood appeafe,

He fhuts his eyes and drops afleep with eafe.

Yet e'en this madman runs no rifks for fame,

Tho' youth encourage, and tho' wine inflame.

The purple cloak, the num'rous train, the light

Of brazen lamps that diffipate the night,

And pour a fplendor thro' the darken'd ftreets,

He marks afar and prudently retreats ;

But I who wander by the lunar ray,

Or with a farthing candle grope my way ;

Whofe quiv'ring flame I tend with anxious care,

And ftrive to guard it from the rufhing air,

---

* *Pope's Iliad, B.* 24.

Contemnit.   Miferæ cognofce prooemia rixæ.

Si rixa eft, ubi tu pulfas, ego vapulo tantum.

Stat contra, ftarique jubet ; parere neceffe eft :

Nam quid agas, cum te furiofus cogat, et idem

Fortior ? unde venis ? exclamat : cujus aceto,

Cujus conche, tumes ? quis tecum fectile porrum

Sutor et elixi vervecis labra comedit ?

Nil mihi refpondes ? aut dic, aut accipe calcem :

Ede ubi confiftas ? in qua te quæro profeucha ?

Dicere fi tentes aliquid, tacitufve recedas,

Tantundem eft : feriunt pariter : vadimonia deinde

Irati faciunt : libertas pauperis hæc eft,

I ſuffer; as the coward ruffian knows,

His rage, I neither can nor dare oppoſe—

The conteſt thus begins; if conteſt call'd,

Where he deals blows, and I alone am maul'd

Stand villain, ſtand, he cries, and blocks my way;

He's drunk and ſtronger and I muſt obey,

Speak, where have you been drinking muſty lees?

What cobler ſtrove your lordſhip's taſte to pleaſe,

With ſheep's head and with onions pounded ſmall

Say, in what beggar's nook for alms you bawl?

In what dark cell or cave at night you lie?

Nay quick, or take this kick or give reply.

Whether in ſilent fear you ſeek retreat,

Or try to ſpeak, 'tis juſt the ſame, they beat,

And juſtice then in mighty wrath demand,

And ſwear by you the whole affair was plann'd.

Such, ſuch the freedom that we wretches know,

And ſuch the mercy our ſuperiors ſhow;

Pulfatus rogat, et pugnis concifus adorat,

Ut liceat paucis cum dentibus inde reverti.

Nec tamen hoc tantum metuas : nam qui fpoliet te

Non deerit, claufis domibus, poftquam omnis ubique

Fixa catenatæ filuit compago tabernæ.

Interdum et ferro fubitus graffator agit rem,

Armato quoties tutæ cuftode tenentur

Et Pontina palus et Gallinaria pinus.

Sic inde huc omnes, tanquam ad vivaria, currunt.

Quâ fornace graves, quâ non incude, catenæ ?

Forgivenefs we, when injur'd muft implore,

Muft pray when menac'd, and when ftruck adore;

And when the tyrant's wrath fatigu'd we find,

Muft thank him, that he leaves a tooth behind.

Nor, e'en if treated thus you fcape at laft,

Difmifs all fears and think all dangers paft.

When noify fhops their midnight labors clofe,

And all exhaufted feek a fhort repofe,

Then fecret robbers fteal upon your reft,

Pick ev'ry lock and rifle ev'ry cheft;

Perhaps, determin'd to fecure the prize,

Plunge the fwift dagger and prevent your cries.

Chac'd from their haunts the ruffians hither fly

Convinc'd that Rome will work and food fupply—

So vaft the number of thefe nightly foes,

With bolts and fhackles ev'ry furnace glows—

Maximus in vinclis ferri modus, ut timeas, ne

Vomer deficiat, ne marræ et farcula defint.

Felices proavorum atavos, felicia dicas

Sæcula, quæ quondam fub regibus atque tribunis

Viderunt uno contentam carcere Romam.

His alias poteram et plures fubnectere caufas :

Sed jumenta vocant et fol inclinat ; eundum eft :

Nam mihi commotâ jam dudum mulio virgâ

Adnuit : ergo vale noftri memor ; et quoties te

Roma tuo refici properantem reddet Aquino,

The mines are wasted, and there's cause to fear

A want of rakes and shares will soon appear.

How blest our ancestors; how blest the times

That fear'd no tyrants, and that knew no crimes.

When Rome, beneath her kings and tribunes reign,

Saw one small jail her criminals contain.

Much could I add, more reasons could I cite,

To justify my hate, and urge my flight—

But now the wasted time forbids delay,

The sun declining shoots a feebler ray,

The driver cracks his whip and summons me away.

Farewell, my friend, farewell; yet ere we part,

I charge you bear me mindful in your heart;

And oft as you from hated Rome repair,

To breath your own Aquinum's purer air,

H

Me quoque ad Helvinam Cererem veftramque Dianam
Convelle a Cumis : fatyrarum ego, ni pudet illas,
Adjutor gelidos veniam caligatus in agros,

From Cumæ, in my ruſtic garb array'd,

I'll ſeek your bleak abode ; and if my aid

Your muſe allow, aſſiſt your virtuous rage,

And rouſe juſt horror at an impious age.

NOTES, &c.

From the copious and learned obfervations of Mr. Gifford, I have extracted a few notes, which feemed neceffary to render the poem intelligible, to the mere Englifh reader. A few paffages, which that gentleman has tranflated, I have omitted; and there are alfo a few to which I have ventured to give an interpretation different from that which he has adopted. I truft the reader will not do me the injuftice to fuppofe that I wifh to be confidered as the opponent or rival of that celebrated writer. His tranflation of Juvenal is doubtlefs unequal, and in fome places perhaps erroneous; yet, notwithftanding the malignant ftrictures of the Critical Reviewers and their abfurd preference of the very inferior verfion of Mr. Marfh, it certainly deferves to be confidered a mafterly performance; a performance to which, of all living writers he alone was probably equal. The

verfification, tho' fometimes harſh or licentious, is
generally fpeaking, free, varied, and harmonious ; yet,
in contradiction to the tafte of moſt readers, partaking
more of the energy and flow of Dryden, than the
melody and concifeneſs of Pope.   Engliſh readers will
no longer be referred to the admirable imitations of
Dr. Johnſon, as the only fources whence they can de-
rive a juſt idea of the manner and fpirit of the Roman
Satiriſt ; the peculiar characteriſtics of the poet, his
dignity, his vehemence, his profound horror of vice,
his burſts of uncontroulable indignation are happily
and almoſt uniformly preferved in the tranflation of
Mr. Gifford ; the figures are fo well defined, the
colors fo vivid, and the expreffion fo ftrongly marked,
that without injuſtice we cannot apply to this tranflation the celebrated and happy metaphor of Cervantes ;
we cannot call it " the wrong fide of the tapeſtry"—
I fhould indeed poffeſs an abundant portion of that vanity with which we are reproached as a national vice,
fhould I dare for a moment to think of entering the
lifts with fuch a poet as Mr. Gifford.   I had no fuch
thought, the prefent tranflation was written merely as
an exercife in the art of verfification.   Were I in
England it fhould not be publifhed, but as an American production and iffuing from an American prefs, I
was willing to believe that it was entitled to fome in-

dulgence. I was alfo defirous to prove that it was poffible for an American to write poetry at leaft with fimplicity and purity ; without recurring to the aid of barbarous and unauthorifed terms, unmeaning or extravagant epithets, harfh or inconfiftent metaphors.

Ver. 4th. " And with one citizen, &c." I have in this line adopted the explication of Mr. Gifford, the fenfe of the original feems to have been ftrangely miftaken by former tranflators.

Ver. 5th " To Baiæ Cumæ leads, &c." The introduction of this circumftance would probably appear to moft readers impertinent; but Mr. Gifford has happily explained the allufion. The commentators not conceiving that the epithet " vacuæ" could with propriety be applied to a place which the poet afterwards defcribes as the thoroughfare to Baiæ, and defirous to fave the veracity of their author, chofe to divert the word from its proper meaning, and explain it by " otiofæ, quietæ, non tam plenæ hominum quam " eft Roma, &c." but of thefe Mr. Gifford obferves there is no need, " a place may be uninhabited though " numbers pafs through it daily, and this in truth, is " what the author fatirically hints at; that Baiæ, " which Seneca calls " diverforium vitiorum," fhould " have fuch attractions for the Romans, as to draw

" them all to it, in despite of the many delightful
" spots in its vicinity, through which they were obli-
" ged to pass, and of whose charms, therefore, they
" could not be ignorant."

Ver. 14.   " When *raving poets seize you and recite.*"
The following passage may perhaps occur to the reader :

Fire in each eye, and papers in each hand,
They rave, recite, and madden round the land.
POPE's Pro. to the Sab.

And the still more humorous lines with which Horace
concludes the " Epistola ad Pisones."

Indoctum doctumque fugat recitator acerbus
Quem vero adripuit, tenet, occiditque legendo.

I am inclined to think that both passages must have
been present to my mind, when I wrote the above line,
though at the time, however strange it may seem, I
was unconscious of the fact—Indeed I am convinced,
that many of the imitations pointed out by bishop
Hurd, in his admirable essay, on the " Marks of imitation in Poetry," were of this nature—That the authors were secretly influenced in the choice of senti-
ment or expression, by an indistinct recollection of the
passages, which he supposes them designedly to have

copied. Martial has addreffed to one of thefe " recitanteis poetæ," a very humorous epigram : after having perufed it, the reader will not be furprifed that
Juvenal has placed them in the climax of the evils
with which Rome was infefted.

Occurrit tibi nemo quòd libenter :
Quòd quacunque venis fuga eft, et ingens
Circa te, Ligurine, folitude :
Quid fit fcire cupis ? nimis poëta es.
Nam tantos, rogo, quis ferat labores ?
Et ftanti legis, et legis fedenti :
Currenti legis, et legis canenti.
In thermas fugio : fonas ad aurem.
Pifcinam peto : non licet natare.
Ad cœnam propero : tenes euntem.
Ah cœnam venio : fugas fedentem.
Laffus dormio : fufcitas jacentem.
Vis, quantum facias mali, videre ?
Vir juftus, probus, innocens timeris.

You're anxious then, my worthy friend, to know
Why, when you enter, all prepare to go ?
Why, when you walk, all claffes fhun to meet,
And folitude ufurps the crowded ftreet ?
You are, and all who once have met you know it,
You are, my worthy friend, too much a poet.

A dang'rous fault, which, truft me, you fhould cure,
For who, the toils you afk, could e'er endure?
Howe'er engag'd I feem, by day or night,
Heedlefs of time and place, you ftill recite.
I feek the baths, but follow'd ftill by you;
I fly to Tibur, and you ftill purfue;
If I to fupper hafte, my courfe you ftay;
If I at fupper fit, you drive away;
Wearied to death, I fink, with fleep oppreft;
You raife your voice, nor give a moment's reft.
Your hands, we own, are pure, your confcience clear;
We all refpect you, but alas, we fear.

Ver. 18. " And Numa nightly, &c." Livy tells us, that, juft without the walls of Rome, there was a little grove, watered by a perennial fpring, which rofe in the middle of it. To this, Numa, who had probably contracted, in the privacy of his former life, a love of folitude, which followed him to the throne, ufed frequently to retire: and here he feems, foon after his acceffion, to have conceived the defign of turning his darling propenfity to the advantage of his new fubjects. For this purpofe, he gave out, that, in this lonely recefs, he met the goddefs Egeria, who furnifhed him from time to time, with the ftatutes to be obferved by the city. A rude, and uninformed race of warriors liftened with awe to the dictates of Heaven:

and Numa had the satisfaction of feeling his institutions not merely received, but revered. Livy's description is so pleasing, that I cannot withhold it from the classical reader.

" Lucus erat, quem medium ex opaco specu fons per-
" enni rigabat aqua, quo quia se persæpe Numa,
" sine arbitris, velut ad congressum Deæ, inferebat ;
" Camœnis eum lucum sacravit quod earum ibi con-
" silia cum conjuge sua Egeria essent."

Verse 25. ———————" Sure the nymph would seem
    Far, far more present if her gurgling stream," &c.
Mr. Mason in a note to his " English Garden" quotes these lines as an honorable proof, that Juvenal was uninfected by the corrupt taste of the age in which he lived. The lines which Mr. Gifford has quoted from Ovid, show that he is entitled to a similar praise. It is a circumstance worthy of remark that both Cicero and Pliny were great admirers of the factitious and unnatural taste which the two poets so warmly reprobate (See a note on the first book of the E. Garden).

The following is the " exquisite description" of Ovid which Juvenal has so happily copied. The translation is by a friend.

" ———In extremo est antrum nemorale recessu;
" Arte laboratum nullâ ; simulaverat artem

" Ingenio natura fuo : nam pumice vivo,
" Et levibus tophis nativum duxerat arcum,
" Fons fonat à dextrâ tenui perlucidus undâ,
" Margine gramineo patulos fuccinctus hiatus.

Deep in the vale a fhady grot there lies,
Where nature's charms, untouch'd by art, furprize ;
For there, the Genius of the place alone
The pebbles rang'd and arch'd the living ftone ;
There, on the right, a bubbling fount is feen,
Of lucid wave, and bank of frefheft green.

Verfe 61.   " What fhould I do at Rome I cannot
lie, &c."   One of Martial's beft epigrams bears a
ftrong refemblance to this paffage of our author.   My
friend has again obliged me with a tranflation.   The
claffical reader will find a ftill better epigram on the
fame fubject.   Lib. 3, 28.

Ad Fabianum.

Vir bonus et pauper, linguaque et pectore verus,
   Quid tibi vīs, urbem qui Fabiane petis ?
Qui nec leno potes nec commiffator haberi,
   Nec pavidos, trifti voce, citare reos :
Nec potes uxorem cari corrumpere amici :
   Nec potes algentes arrigare ad vetulas
Vendere nec vanos circa Palatia fumos :
   Plaudere nec Cano, plaudere nec Glaphyro,

Unde miſer vives ; homo fidus, certus amicus,
   Hoc nihil eſt ; nunquam ſic * Philomelus eris.

Honeſt and poor, in word and thought ſincere,
What buſineſs tell me, haſt thou Fabian, here ?
The pimp or flatt'rers trade thou canſt not ply,
Nor on thy pow'rs can aged dames rely.
Canſt thou to mean and ſordid gain deſcend ?
Corrupt the wife of him who calls thee friend ?
The gaping crowd with empty hopes deceive ?
Or low buffoons accompliſh'd players believe ?
If not how live at Rome ? What thou art juſt,
Wilt not deſert thy friend, and break thy truſt ?
Fly, if thou wouldſt not ſtarve, the walls of Rome,
And ſeek again thy quiet ruſtic home ;
To virtues ſuch as theſe we ſhow no grace,
They ne er will give you bread, or gain you place.

Ver. 65. " I ne'er have learnt the virtues of the
toad, &c." Frequent alluſions are found in ancient
authors to the poiſonous qualities of the toad : but
" either our toad is not the rana rubeta of the ancients, or it has loſt its deſtructive qualities in this
country ; where it is generally underſtood to be al-

---

* Philomelus was a celebrated player on the harp who
had amaſſed an immenſe fortuue.

together innoxious. It is frequently alluded to by Pliny, and once in strong terms, as extremely hostile to life. The compounders of these doses, (and, as Rabelais says, there was a world of people at Rome then, as well as now, that got an honest livelihood by poisoning) might probably give out such a report, to conceal the real fact; but I should imagine the substances they used were either vegetable, or mineral, and of a much more subtle, and deleterious nature than any thing the genus of toads could supply. It is no great reflection, however, on our author, that he was ignorant of the secret."

GIFFORD.

Ver. 83. " Him who arraigns when Verres self thinks fit, &c."

Q. Cæcilius who had been Verres' quæstor in Sicily, and the accomplice of his crimes, demanded, for very obvious reasons, to be preferred, as his accuser, to Cicero—Hortensius, who defended Verres, was at that time Consul elect; and M. Metellus, who was also strangely attached to his interest, had been designated Prætor. Had Cæcilius been chosen the accuser, it was intended that the trial of Verres should be deferred until these magistrates had entered on the execution of their duties; and in this case the acquittal of the criminal was considered as certain. (Vide in Q. Cæ-

cilium Div. et in Verrem Actio Pri. cap. 8.———)
which contains an account of a very curious negotia-
tion (as the phrafe is) the object of which was to defeat
the election of Cicero as Ædile. Some perfons pretend that in all countries and in all ages elections have
been conducted in very nearly a fimilar manner; but
in this country it feems we have found the fecret of
enjoying all the advantages of a popular government,
unalloyed by any portion of the evils. Who fhall
dare to fay, that in this *virtuous* and enlightened country the freedom of elections has ever been impaired, or
their purity polluted?

Ver. 99.————————" O Romulus behold,
      See foreign robes thy ruftic now infold."

In this apoftrophe to Romulus the poet obferves that
while the Greeks, &c. were worming themfelves into
all places of power and profit, the Romans once fo
renowned for their rough and manly virtues, were
wholly taken up with the idle amufements of the Circus. Niceteria are prizes which the victors, in the
contefts of the Circus, oftentatioufly wore round their
necks. And Ceroma is a mixture of oil, clay, and
bees-wax, with which the wreftlers fmeared their
neck and breafts.

GIFFORD.

Ver. 116. " And bid him go to heav'n, to heav'n
he goes."

The poet here alludes to the flight of Dædalus;
and prefently after explains himfelf more fully, by ob-
ferving that it was no barbarian who mad!y attempt-
ed a flight through the air; but a Greek mediis natus
Athenis.   He artfully adduces this inftance to prove,
that the prefum,tion and avarice of the Greeks would
lead them to any, the moft extravagant undertakings.

Ver. 181. "Extol the learning of the unlearn'd friend."
Great indeed muft have been the fkill of the Greeks,
if they could fucceed by this method of flattery—A
very oppofite courfe is recommended by a modern mafter of the art.

Would you by flatt'ry feek the road to wealth?
Pufh not too hard; but flide it in by ftealth.
Mark well your cully's temper and purfuit.
And fit to ev'ry leg the pliant boot.
Tell not the fpendthrift that he hoards with fenfe,
Tell not the mifer that he fcorns expence.
Nor praife the learning of a dunce profeft,
Nor fwear a floven's elegantly dreft.

Still let your lies to truth near neighbors be,
And ftill with probability agree.

        " Ars mentiendi," of Lord H. Spencer.

Ver. 141. " The wife, the miftrefs, and the un-
    dreft fair," &c.

The characters of women in ancient times, were always reprefented by men. It was not until the reign
of Charles the fecond, if I am not miftaken, that women were introduced on the Englifh ftage.

Ver. 144. " The patron laughs—a louder laugh
    replies."

The character of the flatterer is touched with great
force in thefe lines, which are however, exceeded,
at leaft in humour, by the following :

Hamlet. Your bonnet to its right ufe : 'tis for the head.

Ofrick. I thank your lordfhip 'tis very hot.

Hamlet. No, believe me, 'tis very cold, the wind is
    northerly.

Ofrick. It is indifferently cold, my lord, indeed.

Hamlet. But yet, methinks, it is very fultry and hot
    for my complexion.

Ofrick. Exceedingly, my lord, it is very fultry as it were, I can t tell how.

GIFFORD.

Ver. 149. " They fhiver and their fhaggy cloaks require." Accipit endromidem. The endromis or endro.nida was a thick, fhaggy cloak, chiefly ufed in the Gymnafia, and put on by the wreftlers, runners, &c. after the perfor.nance of their violent exercifes to prevent the effects of a fudden chill. Martial has an epigram, (Lib. 4, ep. 19) in which he defcribes its origin and various ufes ; he concludes with faying :

" Ridebis ventos hoc munere tectu; et imbres."
In this involv d the winds and rain defy.

Ver. 166. " Yon ftoic mark, &c."
This is meant for P. Ægnatius who appeared againft his patron and friend Bareas Soranus accused of a confpiracy againft Nero. Tacitus (who defcribes the whole tranfaction) after a very pathetic account of the accufation of Soranus and his daughter by Oftorius Sabinus, procee ds to defcribe in his ftrong and impref-five language the indignation caufed by the treachery of Ægnatius ; " Mox datus teftibus locus et quantum miferecordiæ fævitia accufationis permoverat, tantum iræ P· Egnatius teftis concivit. Cliens hic Sorani, et tunc emptus ad opprimendum amicum, auctorita-

tem Stoicæ fectae praeferebat, habitu et ore ad ex-
pri endum imaginem honefti exercitus, ceterùm an-
i o perfidiofus, fubdolus, avaritiam ac libidinem oc-
cultans. Quæ poftquam pecuniâ reclufa funt, dedit
exemplum praecavendi, quomodo fraudibus involutos,
aut flagitiis commaculatos, fic fpecie bonarum artium
falfos, et amicitiae fallaces.

Tac. Ann. Lib. 16, 32.

Ver. 169. " Where the wing'd hack," &c.
Tarfus in Cilicia, where Pegafus was faid to have ftumbled, and dropt a feather from his fetlock. He terms
Pegafus a hack not (as Cafaubon obferves) from a
contempt of him whom the ancients had placed in heaven; but becaufe he mortally hated the Greeks.

GIFFORD.

Ver. 178. " Trifling indeed; for why the truth
deny, &c."
This (Mr. Gifford obferves) is touched with great force
by Martial. The following is the epigram (perhaps
the beft in Martial) to which Mr. Gifford refers. It
will not, I am confident, be faid that the fpirit of the
original has evaporated in the tranflation of my friend.

In Paulum.

Confulem et Salutatorem.

Cum tu laurigeris annum qu. fafcibus in ras,

Manê falutator limina mille teras :
Hic ego quid fa.iam ? quid nobis Paulle relinquis,
   Qui de plebe Numa, denfaque turba fumus ?
Qui me refpiciat, dominum regemque vocabo ?
   Hoc tu, fed quanto blandiùs, ipfe facis.
Lecticam, feliamque fequar ? nec ferre recufo :
   Per medium pugnas fed prior ire lutum.
S. pius affurgam recitanti carmina ? tu ftas,
   Et pariter geminas tendis in ora manus.
Quid faciat pauper, cui non licet effe clienti ?
   Dimifit noftras purpura veftra togas.

When you, whom riches birth and rank adorn,
Salute a thoufand portals in a morn ;
What muft I do ? Say Paulus what remains
To us, the wretched crowd, whom this fuftains ?
To gain the patron's fmile, or gracious nod,
I ll call him, if he pleafe, a king or god ;
But then you praife, with fuch fuperior art,
He frowns on me and gives to you his heart ;
Shall I on foot attend the patron's chair ?
It nought avails ; for ftill I find you there.
You rufh the foremoft of the fervile train,
Dafh thro the mud, nor heed the beating rain.
What fhould the patron choofe his verfe recite ?
I rife, and lift my hands, and feign delight ;

But you ne'er fit, your hands perpetual raife,
And fhow your extafy a thoufand ways.
Our coarfe and humble gowns no longer dare
Contend, ye nobles, wi h the purple's glare ;
At length, the poor have loft their laft refource,
Difmifs d as clients, we muft ftarve of courfe.

Ver. 196. ——————————" Not the hoft
 Of Cybele could brighter virtue boaft."

In the 54th year of Rome the Sibylline books, being
confulted concerning the expiation of certain prodi-
gies, directed that the goddefs Cybele fhou'd be brought
to Rome, from Peffinus in Phrygia. Ambaffadors
were accordingly fent to king Attalus to procure the
facred ftone, which was dignified with the name of
" Mother of the Gods." The ambaffadors, in their
way to Afia, confulted the Delphic oracle, and were
commanded to lodge the goddefs, on their return to
Rome, with the moft virtuous man in the city ; and
this " moft virtuous man" was determined by the
Senate to be Scipio Naffica. Speaking of this judg-
ment of the Senate, Livy, with his ufual eloquence,
obferves, " Haud parvæ rei judicium Senatum tene-
bat, qui vir optimus in civitate effet. Veram certè
victoriam ejus rei quifque fibi mallet, quam ulla imperia
honorefve, fuffragio feu Patrum feu plebis delatos.

P. Scipionem, Cn. filium, ejus qui in Hispania ceci-
derat, adolescentem nondum quaestorium, judicave-
runt in tota civitate virum bonorum optimum esse.

Lib. 27. c. 14.

Ver. 198. " Nor he who rush'd intrepid thro'
the fire," &c.

This was L. Metellus, Pontifex Maximus, who, in a
dreadful conflagration which happened at Rome a few
years before the last mentioned event, when the fire
had seized the temple of Vesta, and the virgins de-
serted it, ventured his life to save the Palladium. One
of his arms was disabled in the attempt, and his sight
totally destroyed, yet he effected his purpose. Ovid
has some pretty lines on the subject. Fast. 6, 444.

GIFFORD.

The following are the lines to which Mr. Gifford
alludes, and surely they are something more than
pretty. The annexed translation is by no means lit-
teral, indeed the last eight lines are more properly an
imitation.

Heu, quantum timuere Patres quo tempore Vesta
    Arsit, et est adytis obruta penè suis ;
Flagrabant sancti sceleratis ignibus ignes
    Mixtaque erat flammae flamma profana pix.
Attonitae flebant demisso crine ministræ ;

Abftulerat vires corporis ipfe timor.

Provolat in medium, et magna, " fuccurrite," voce,
 " Non eft auxilium flere," Metellus ait,
" Pignora virgineis fatalia tollite palmis ;
 " Non ea funt voto, fed rapienda manu.
" Me mifeum dubitatis ? ' ait, dubitare videbat,
 Et pavidas pofito procubuiffe genu.
Haurit aquas : tollenfque manus, " ignofcite," dixit,
 " Sacra : vir intrabo non adeunda viro.
" Si fcelus eft, in me commiffi poena redundet ;
 " Sit capitis damno Roma foluta mei."
Dixit et irrupit : factum Dea rapta probavit :
 Pontificifque fui munere tecta fuit.

                         Faft. lib. 6. v. 437, 455.

What boding fears the chiefs of Rome difmay'd,
What time the flames on Vefta's temple prey'd,
And fought the goddef' fhrine, and dread abode ;
And midft pure fires with fires unholy glow'd.
Oppreft by woe, and feiz'd with horrid dread,
The virgins feel their ftrength and courage fled :
When Rome's high-prieft in voice of thunder cries,
" To weep is not to fave, ye virgins rife,
" Quick let the fatal pledge be hence convey'd ;
" Your hands alone, and not your pray'rs can aid.
" What ftill unmov'd ?" Unmov'd he fees them ftill ;
Depriv'd by fear, of motion, voice, and will.

" If, goddef, in thy fhrine I dare intrude,
" Thy facred fhrine, which man ne'er yet has view'd,
" And thou fhouldft deem the generous zeal profane,
" On me alone, thy gather'd vengeance rain ;
" Let Rome be fav'd ; is all my vows require."
He faid, and rufhing thro' the circling fire,
The pledge from flames and Rome from ruin freed,
And gods and men approv'd th' heroic deed.

Ver. 206. " Add that the poor continual taunts
provoke," &c.

Dr. Johnfon, in his imitation of this paffage, has fur-
paffed even the fpirit and energy of the original. Often
as the reader may have perufed thefe lines, I am fure
he will not object to my tranfcription of them.

By numbers here, from fhame and cenfure free,
All crimes are fafe but hated poverty ;
This, this alone, the rigid law purfues,
This, this alone, provokes the fnarling mufe ;
The fober trader at a tatter'd cloak
Wakes from his dreams, and labors for a joke ;
With brifker air, the filken courtiers gaze,
And turn the varied taunt a thoufand ways.
Of all the ills that harafs the diftreft,
Sure the moft bitter is a fcornful jeft ;
Fate never wounds fo deep a generous heart
As when a blockhead s infult points the dart.

Ver. 214. "O poverty of all thy numerous ills," &c.
Mr. Gifford has quoted a paffage from Crates, one of
the writers of the old comedy, which contains a thought
very fimilar to this of our author ; not having found a
tranflation of this fragment in the very entertaining
collection, with which Mr. Cumberland has embellifh-
ed the pages of the Obferver, the reader will excufe the
following attempt.

Of all the ills that wretched man afflict,
The ills of poverty fure gall the moft ;
Let nature form you awful, wife, fevere,
Yet poverty fhall change you to a fool,
And make the butt of ridicule and fcorn.

Or in rhyme thus:

Of all the ills we wretched mortals know,
Sure poverty is charg'd the moft with woe ;
Tho' nature with her nobleft gifts adorn,
If poor you're doom'd to ridicule and fcorn.

Notwithftanding this fentiment has been adopted by
Juvenal and improved by Johnfon, I muft be allowed
to queftion its juftnefs. In the breaft of him who
poffeffes a proper confcioufnefs of his own merit, and
a true fenfe of his own dignity, the laugh of fools can
excite no emotions but thofe of pity and contempt.

K

Ver. 218. Quit, quit thofe benches, angry Lectius
    cries, &c.

In the 685th year of the city, L. Otho procured a law,
by which feparate feats in the theatres, were affigned
to the knights.   This diftinction, which was exceedingly odious to the poorer claffes at Rome, had been lately
revived by Domitian and overfeers appointed to enforce
its obfervance.   Martial gives us the name of one of
thefe officers.

    " Quadringenta tibi non funt, Chæreftrate, furge,
    " LECTIUS ecce venit : fta, fuge, curre, late."

                          Lib. 5, 26.

Ver. 249. " When theatres of turf again they raife, &c."
The Romans had, for a long time, no other than temporary theatres, fo conftructed that the people were obliged to ftand; left, as Tacitus obferves, the convenience
of fitting fhould induce them idly to fpend whole days
at the fpectacle.   They were afterwards contrived more
conveniently ; but continued to be built of light materials, and merely for the occafion, until Pompey erected
a fuperb one of hewn ftone.   It feems, however that
thefe temporary ftructures were fometimes ufed even
in the time of Juvenal.

    " Ovid has a charming picture of the fimplicity of
paft times, in thofe edifices ; which he artfully contrafts

with the luxury and magnificence of the prefent."

"Tunc neque marmoreo pendebant vela theatro." &c.
                        Ars Amandi, lib. 1. v. 103.

" Then, from the marble theatres, no veils
" Wav'd lightly in the fun ; no faffron fhowers
" Bedrench'd the ftage with odours.   Oaken boughs,
" Lopt on the fpot, and rudely rang'd around
" By the glad fwains, a leafy bower compos'd—
" Here 'midft the fimple fcenery, they fat,
" Or on the green-fward, or the flowing turf,
" Artlefsly piled ; while their rough brows were
      crown'd
" With garlands, fuch as the next tree fupplied."
                                    GIFFORD.

Of thefe beautiful lines of Ovid, my friend, for the
fake of the lovers of rhyme, has given me the following tranflation.

No veils were then o'er marble ftructures fpread ;
No liquid odors fhower'd round the head ;
The neareft grove fupplied its choiceft green,
And cluft'ring branches form'd the artlefs fcene ;
Rude feats of turf, in order rofe around ;
Where fate the fwains, with many a garland crown'd.

    Ver.   " E'en then both rich and poor are cloth'd
      alike."

"———————Similemque videbis
Orcheſtram, et populum,"————

In the diviſions of the Roman Theatre (for thoſe of the Greeks were different,) orcheſtra ſignified the place where the dances were performed : it was next the pulpitum or ſtage, but not on a level with it ; and, as affording a good view of the actors, was uſually frequented by the ſenators, who had chairs placed for them there. In his ſeventh ſatire, Juvenal makes his poet borrow thoſe chairs to accommodate his audi-ence at a private houſe :

" Quæque reportandis poſita eſt orcheſtra cathedris."

Our ruſtic theatre had no ſuch orcheſtra of courſe ; and Umbritius here uſes the word figuratively for the ſpace neareſt the actors, where the wealthier villagers ſat.

In the next line the poet purſues the contraſt be-tween the luxury and extravagance of Rome, and the frugality of the country : there the meaneſt of the people aſſiſted at the theatre dreſſed in white ; here the Ædiles only, under whom the plays were acted, and whoſe importance is, according to cuſtom, ironi-cally magnified.

It is ſingular that this ſhould have eſcaped Dryden ;

" ————————clari velamen honoris,
" Sufficiunt tunicæ fummis Ædilibus albæ."

He renders

" In his white cloak the magiftrate appears,
" The country bumpkin the fame livery wears."

Which is directly contrary, not only to the intent, but to the words of his author.

GIFFORD.

Ver. 264.   " A paffing nod fhall haughty Coffus deign."

The original is infinitely more humorous ; Quid das ut Cosfum aliquando falutes ? What will you give that Côsfus may fometimes permit you to falute him ? In defence of my own inaccuracy, I can only plead the example of former tranflators.   It has been fuggefted to me that " falutes" refers to the attendance of the client at the levee ; for which falutare is the appropriate word ; this may poffibly be the cafe, but in no tranflation, that I have feen, is the paffage thus interpreted.

Ver. 268.   " This minion fhaves his head, this lops his hair."

It was cuftom of the wealthier Romans to dedicate the firft fhavings of their beard, and pollings of their hair, after they arrived at a state of manhood to some deity. Thus Suetonius and Dio tell us, among a variety of other instances, that Nero inclosed his in a golden pix, adorned with pearls, and offered it with great state to the Capitoline Jove. The day this was done by the rich, was kept as a festival, and presents were expected from relations, friends, and clients, as on their birth days, &c. This, however, is not what provoked the spleen of Umbritius : he complains, and justly too, that these presents should be exacted from the poor dependant, not only when his patron, but when his patron's minions, first polled and shaved ! He is indignant, that it should be necessary to pay them tribute, as he calls it ; since, possessing the ear of the lord, no means of access were left the client, but through the good pleasure of these proud slaves, which could only be purchased by presents.

GIFFORD.

Ver. 295. "For thus, so wife so provident their care, The inking walls our master stewards repair."

—— — —— —"nam fic labentibus obstat Villicus, et veteris rimæ contexit hiatum."

This seems to me, the most obscure and difficult passage in the whole poem ; it is thus rendered by Mr. Gifford.

" For thus the ftewards patch the river wall,
" Thus prop the manfion, tottering to its fall."

But what ftewards? If this tranflation be correct
I muft own myfelf unable to comprehend the allufion.
By "villicus" I fuppofe, that Juvenal means the prefect
of the city, whom in the following fatire he defignates
by the fame term.

"————attonitæ modo pofitus villicus urbi."

By this interpretation the ftrict eonnexion of the
paffage with what precedes becomes evident.

Ver. 308. ———— ———— ————" nor ftill you wake,
For, fince its ravages begin below,
Your garret laft the raging peft will know."

" Tu nefcis ; nam fi gradibus trepidatur ab imis,
Ultimus ardebit," &c.

The paffage is given thus by Mr. Gifford :

"———— — ———— up, ho ! and know
That when th' impetuous peft begins below,
The topmoft ftory foon becomes its prey," &c.
But this is certainly wrong, the meaning of Juvenal is,
that the height of the houfes was fo great, that the un-
fortunate tenant of the garret might be wrapt in fleep,

while the ftories below were in flames. The words
"nam fi gradibus trepidatur ab imis," &c. are expla-
natory of " tu nefcis." The conjunction " nam",
which (as it is always caufative) clearly proves this to be
the cafe, is omitted in the tranflation of Mr. Gifford.

Ver. 310. " Juftice is ftaid, the matron rends her
hair,".

We have here a very accurate defcription of a public
mourning for any fignal calamity. The women laid
afide their ornaments ; the fenate put on black ; the
courts of juftice deferred all bufinefs, &c. That all
this would be done on fuch an occafion as the prefent,
may be reafonably doubted ;—and yet if we duly attend to the ftate of Rome in our authors time, we
fhall not be inclined to fufpect him of much exaggeration ; for to be rich and childlefs gave the perfon fo
circumftanced the utmoft confequence.

GIFFORD.

Ver. 324. " And all fufpect him author of the
fire."

Martial has the fame thought on a fimilar event, expreffed with no lefs elegance and brevity.

" Empta domus fuerat tibi, Tongiliane, ducentis :
   " Abftulit hanc nimium cafus in urbe frequens.

" Collatum eſt decies. Rogo, non potes ipſe videri
" Incendiſſe tuam, Tongiliane, domum ?"

The ſingular art with which the poet contraſts the
different fates of Codrus and Aſturius, has not, I truſt,
eſcaped the notice of the reader ; any more than the
dexterity with which it is made conducive to the great,
Indeed the ſole, object of the ſatire.

GIFFORD.

Ver. 340. "'Tis ſomething e'en one lizard to poſſeſs."
" We aſked Dr. Johnſon" (ſays Boſwell, in his amu-
ſing life of that author) " the meaning of that expres-
ſion in Juvenal, *unius dominum lacertæ.* Johnſon, I
think it clear enough ; it means as much ground as
one may have a chance of finding a lizard upon."
And ſo it does ! and this, the Doctor might have
added, is very little in Italy.

GIFFORD.

Ver. 343. " In ſilent anguiſh rolls his ſleepleſs eyes."

In the following quotation, the reader will recog-
nize the " energy" of Lucretius ; it is taken from his
deſcription of the plague at Athens.

Quippe patentia cùm totas ardentia nocteis
Lumina verſarent occulorum expertia ſomn

For their broad eye-balls, burning with difeafe
Roll'd in full ftare, forever void of fleep.

GOOD.

Ver. 353.   " Whilft as he moves the willing crowd
    gives way.'

We have here another lively picture of the mifery attending the great inequality of fortunes in a ftate fo
conftituted as that of Rome.   The rich rapidly, and
almoft without confcioufnefs of impediment, moving
to the levees of the old and childlefs ; while the poor
whofe fole fupport probably depended upon their early
appearance there, are hopelefsly ftruggling with dangers and difficulties that fpring up at every ftep to re-
tard them.

GIFFORD.

Ver. 360.   " And foldiers hob-nail'd fhoes indent
    my toes."

"— — — — et in digito clavus mihi militis hæret."

The following is Lubin's explanation.   " Id eft cal-
"ceus, multis clavis fuffixus, digito pedis mei infigitur."
Boileau has imitated this whole paffage in his fixth
Satire.

" L'un me heurte d'un ais , dont je fuis tout froiff¿
Et d'un autre coup mon chapeau eft renverfé".   &c.

Ver. 363. " See from the dole what clouds of smoke arife."

The dole, *sportula*, was the portion of meat received by each client who accompanied his patron home from the forum.   The poet obferves, that each of thefe clients was followed by his kitchen, and as it farther appears, preferved fome ftate at home ; it is probable that his view here was to expofe the meannefs and avarice of the rich, who were content to fwell the train of the vain or ambitious, and to exact the dole in confequence of it, to the manifeft injury of the poorer claimants, in whofe favor the diftribution was firft inftituted.

GIFFORD.

Ver. 375.   " Behold that carriage heap'd with maffy ftones.''

This feems to be an oblique attack on the phrenzy of the emperors for building ; as it was chiefly for their ufe, that thefe immenfe beams, maffes of ftone, &c. were brought to Rome.   Juvenal, however, lived to fee the evil, in fome degree, leffened, at leaft, if we may credit Pliny, who celebrates Trajan (Paneg. c. 2) for his moderation in this refpect.   Here is the paffage, and it is a very pertinent one.   He firft commends him for being *tam parcus in ædificando quam diligens in tuendo;* and he immediately adds : *Itaque non ut ante im-*

manium transvectione saxorum urbis tecta quatiuntur :
Stant secura domus, nec jam templa nutantia.

GIFFORD.

Ver. 388. "Without a farthing to get ferried o'er."
The ancients believed, that the souls of the deceased
could not cross the Styx, without paying a trifling fare
to Charon, for their passage ; this they were careful to
put into the mouths of their dead friends, previous to
their being carried out for interment. This idle notion,
the Romans borrowed, together with other fooleries,
from the Greeks : it does not indeed appear to have
been general ; but the vulgar, who every where adopted it, adhered to the custom with the most scrupulous
pertinacity, and feared nothing so much as being con-
signed to the grave without their farthing.

Lucian frequently sneers at this fancy : and our author who, amidst his belief of a future state, had sense
enough to mark the folly of the prevailing system, evidently points his ridicule at the monstrous absurdity
of the practice.

GIFFORD.

Ver. 401. "The drunken bully strives to sleep in vain
        Who seeks, &c."
There is a surprising similarity between this passage,

and one in the Proverbs of Solomon. " Enter not into the path of the wicked, and go not in the way of evil men : for they fleep not except they have done mifchief, and their reft is taken away except they caufe fome to fall." Chap. 4. 14.

The picture which follows ; the humorous, but ftrong and indignant, picture of the miferies to which the poor were expofed by the brutal infolence of debauchees, roaming in queft of objects on whom to exercife their cruelty ; is no exaggeration of our author's ; grave hiftorians have delivered the fame account. Thus Tacitus, in his life of Nero ; who, by the way, appears to have been one of the firft difturbers of the public peace. " In the garb of a flave, he roved thro' the ftreets, attended by a band of rioters, who offered violence to all that fell in their way. In thefe mad frolics he was fometimes wounded ;" not with impunity, however, for it appears that Julius Montanus was put to death, for repelling his infults.

GIFFORD.

Ver. 468. ———————" In my ruftic garb array'd." In the interpretation of the word *caligatus*, I follow the opinion of Mr. Ireland, who fuppofes " *caliga* to mean a country fhoe, as diftinguifhed from a town fhoe." This interpretation confifts with the general drift of the fatire, and the preference which Umbritius

L

gives, in every inftance, to the country. The con-
cluding obfervations of Mr. Gifford, are conceived
with tafte and exprefled with elegance and precifion.
" There is fomething, he remarks, exquifitely beautiful
in the conclufion of this fatire ; the little circumftan-
ces which accelerate the departure of Umbritius, the
tender departure of his friend, the compliment he in-
troduces to his abilities, and the affectionate hint he
throws out, that in fpite of his attachment to Cumæ,
he may command his affiftance in the noble tafk in
which he is engaged, all contribute to leave a pleafing
impreffion of melancholy on the mind, and intereft
the reader deeply in the fate of this neglected, but
virtuous and amiable afcetic."

ADDITIONAL NOTES.

Ver. 53. " Him who arraigns when Verres felf
thinks fit," &c.
" Carus erit Verri qui Verrem tempore, quo vult
" Accufare poteft."

I am afraid no commentator will juftify the translation I have given of this paffage. The following is the note of Lubin : " qui novit Verrem furem

effe illum Verres in fummo pretio, quamvis invitus habebit : timebit. ne ab illo prodatur," and the translation of Mr. Gifford, conveys the fame idea. Yet as I have had the temerity to give a new interpretation, I may as well attempt to fupport it : In the firft place I am inclined to believe that the phrafe " quo tempore" always refers to fome particular period, and is never ufed indefinitely. We cannot therefore tranflate the fentence, " He who can accufe Verres, *at any* " *time* that he may think proper, &c." but muft neceffarily render it : " He who will accufe Verres at " that particular time, when Verres himfelf wifhes to " be accufed," &c. alluding to that historical anecdote which I have given in the former note on this verfe. In the next place, I think this interpretation is more confiftent with the general purport of the paffage, the fubftance of which may be thus compreffed : " At " Rome the poor are almoft entirely dependant on the " great, how then fhould I continue to live there, who " neither know, nor would practice the arts by which " alone their favor is to be acquired. Honorable fer- " vices meet with no remuneration ; he alone who will " affift them to commit or conceal their crimes, may " hope to fhare their wealth ; but however great and " tempting be the reward, do not at the expence of the " peace and tranquility of your mind, purchafe a favor " fo precarious and fo dangerous."

Ver. 193.   "Nor dare to hand the wanton from her feat."

Ladies of a certain defcription at Rome, were accuftomed to feat themfelves on lofty chairs, that the adorers, who approached, might have a fuller and more leifurely view of their charms; or in the coarfe language of Ferrarius: "Ut accedentes fcortatores vena"lem mercem attentiùs confiderarent."

Ver. 453.   "That fear'd no tyrants, and that knew no crimes."

This language is too bold, it may be faid, even for Juvenal to have employed, and I muft own that it cannot be juftified by the letter of his text: yet I am convinced from his allufion to the mode of government which prevailed in thofe early and happy ages, that he meant to fuggeft the comparifon, which I have openly expreffed. In confirmation of my opinion, I find that Rigaltius in his differtation "De Satyra Juvenalis" quotes this paffage, amongft others, in proof of the erect and independent fpirit of the Satirift; they do indeed difcover, (as he expreffes it,) "ingens retinendæ "libertatis defiderium."

ORIGINAL POEMS.

LINES ADDRESSED TO MISS ***** ******

NOW warm, Apollo, with the Poet's fire
A youth, who ne'er has touch'd the Mufe's lyre ;
Unform'd by art, and uninfpired by love,
Ne'er taught his words in meafur'd ftrains to move :
O aid him now with fkill, to hold the rein,
He ne'er will mount your Pegafus again.
While to the God, I thus addrefs'd my pray'r,
A fudden voice I heard, or feem'd to hear :
Prefumptuous youth, reftrain awhile thy flight,
Be ftill content to read, ftill fear to write ;
Yet if the Fair command the votive lay,
Attend, and what the God fhall dictate, fay.

O may thy modeſt worth, ſweet girl, ſoon find
Its beſt, its ſole reward, a kindred mind ;
May ſome bleſt youth (repreſs all vain alarms)
Have ſenſe to know, and heart to feel thy charms ;
Then ſhall thy virtues all their force diſplay,
Then ſhow conſpicuous in their brighteſt day.
I ſee thee now, the mother and the wife,
Grace all the duties of domeſtic life ;
With looks of love, yet mix'd with gentle awe,
I ſee the little circle round thee draw.
Thy precepts all, an eaſy entrance find,
And grave indelibly the tender mind.
What care to guard their unſuſpecting youth !
What ſkill to guide their infant thoughts to truth !
If chance, while thus engag'd, thy lord ſurpriſe,
Joy ſwells his heart, and lightens from his eyes ;
With grateful love he ſtrains thee to his breaſt :
Above all riches and all triumphs bleſt—
He ceas'd t' inſpire ; the mind no longer glows,
Reduc'd henceforward to mere humble proſe.

LINES TO THE

MEMORY OF COWPER.

O Bard, of all that ever touch'd the lyre,
Sweeteſt and moſt unfortunate ; the heart
Whoſe chords of ſympathy, in uniſon
To thy pathetic ſtrain, with conſcious joy
Forget to vibrate, of nature, virtue,
Truth, ſimplicity, has loſt all reliſh :
The heart, that for thy ſufferings does not bleed ;
That knows thy cruel and peculiar fate,
And is not torn with pangs of trueſt grief ;
To the fell and gloomy ſavage, of blood
Inſatiate, o'er whoſe mind ſelf reigns ſupreme,
Careleſs of others woes, may well belong ;
But inmate of the breaſt, can never be
Which ſocial life has ſoften'd. Happy they
Prevailing Bard, who with congenial ſoul

Thy page peruse ; whofe thoughts, feelings, paffions,

Prompt to thy great bidding move ; as thy mood

Thou chang'ft, and op'ft with fkilful hand the fprings

Whence Poefy her richeft treafures draws,

Now at the follies fmile, and now the guilt

Deplore, of man benighted : as Nature's

Varied fcenes thy magic pencil paints,

And bodies, warm as life, to fancy's view,

*Are partners of thy genuine raptures :

Thrice happy they, if in thy higher flights,

They ftill can follow thee, with wing unflagg'd,

And whilft the foul, exulting, fcorns the ties,

That hold to earth, and ftill by faith upborne,

Afcends, foar with thee fublime. Pure thy heart,

O Cowper, and thy page that purity

Reflects : no fceptic taunts of Ignorance.

* *Thou know'ft my praife of nature, moft fincere,*
And that my raptures are not conjur'd up,
To serve occafions of poetic pomp,
But genuine, and art partner of them all.

Tafk, book I.

The fruit, and Pride, here fhock the pious mind :
Nought here appears, from which th' ingenuous maid
Her modeft eye, with blufh indignant, turns :
But he that can perufe thee, and not feel
The fparks of virtue, e'en though quench'd they feem'd,
Kindle into flame, and mount within him,
Is a wretch forever loft, unworthy.
Of the name of man : Vain were thy terrors,
Or if immortal blifs, ineffable,
Thou doft not now enjoy, the gates of blifs
To all of Adam's race, are ever clos'd.

LINES ADDRESSED TO
THE FASHIONABLE PART OF MY
YOUNG COUNTRYWOMEN.*

—————

Ye blooming nymphs, our country's joy and pride,
Who in the ftream of fafhion thoughtlefs glide :
No modifh lay, no melting ftrain of love
Is here pour'd forth, your tender hearts to move ;
Yet think not envious age infpires the fong,
Rejecting all our earth-born joys as wrong :
Think me no Matron ftern, who would reprefs
Each modern grace, each harmlefs change of drefs ;
But one whofe heart exults to join the band,
Where joy and innocence go hand in hand,

* This and the following pieces fubfcribed L were given
me by the friend who furnished the introductory Letter ;
moft of them have been already published either in the Port
Folio, or the New-York Evening Poft.

One who, while modefty maintains her place,
(That facred charm which heightens every grace)
Complacent fees your robes excel the fnow,
Or borrow colours from the painted bow ;
But dreads the threaten'd hour of virtue's flight,
More than the peftilence which walks by night.
Say, in thofe half rob'd bofoms are there hid,
No thoughts which fhame and purity forbid ?
Why do thofe fine-wrought veils around you play,
Like mifts which fcarce bedim the orb of day ?
What mean thofe carelefs limbs, that confcious air,
At which the modeft blufh, the vulgar ftare ?
Can fpotlefs minds endure the guilty leer,
The fober matron's frowns, the witling's fneer ?
Are thefe the charms which in this age refin'd,
Enfure applaufe, and captivate the mind ?
Are thefe your boafted powers, are thefe the arts
Which kindle love, and chain inconftant hearts ?
Alas, fome angry pow'r, fome demon's fkill
Has wrought this ftrange perverfity of will :

For fure fome foe to innocence beguiles,

When harmlefs doves attempt the ferpent's wiles.

True, fafhion's laws her ready vot'ries fcreen,

And ogling beaux exclaim, Oh goddefs, queen !

But vile the praife and adoration fought,

By arts degrading to each nobler thought ;

A bafe-born love thofe notes of praife infpires,

That incenfe rifes from unhallowed fires.

If deaf while fhame and purity complain,

If reafon's gentle voice be rais'd in vain,

Thofe flowers you cull with fuch inftinctive art,

Shall teach the charms that captivate the heart.

The flaunting tulip you reject with fcorn,

Its hues tho' brilliant as the tints of morn :

But fearch with care, for humbler flowers that bloom

Beneath the grafs, yet fcatter fweet perfume ;

The buds which only half their fweets difclofe,

*You fondly feize ; but leave the full blown rofe.

*The reader who does not perceive the beauty and delicacy
of thefe images, is not qualified to receive much delight
from poetry.   E.

Humble the praife, and trifling the regard,
Which ever wait upon the moral bard;
But there remains a hateful truth unfung
Which burns the cheek, and faulters on the tongue;
And which, if modefty ftill hover round,
Each virgin breaft, with forrow muft confound:
" Thofe graceful modes," thus fay your flattering beaux
" From ancient times and taftes refin'd arofe"
Difgrace not thus the names of Greece and Rome;
Their birth-place muft be fought for nearer home.
Shame! fhame! heart-rending thought! deep finking ftain!
That Britain's and Columbia's fair fhould deign:
Nay, ftrive their native beauties to enhance,
By arts firft taught by proftitutes of France.*

Oh modefty, and innocence! fweet pair
Of dove-like fifters! ftill attend our fair.

---

* Dr. Barrow in his Treatife on Education, vol. 2, p.
305, fays, " Our young women are probably little aware
" that the fashionable nakednefs of the prefent day, was
" firft adopted in this country in imitation of the revo-
" lutianary proftitutes of France."

Teach them, without your heavn'ly influence,
How vain the charms of beauty, or of fenfe,
Inveft them with your radiance, mild, yet bright,
And give their fparkling eyes a fofter light :
Enchanting dimples on their cheeks beftow,
And bid them with a purer red to glow :
Let winning fmiles too, round thofe dimples gleam,
Like fportive moon-beams, o'er the curling ftream ;
And if refentment on the mufe attend,
From thofe fhe loves, and truly would befriend :
Tell them how cruel and unjuft their ire,
How pure the feelings, which thefe lays infpire :
How oft fhe fighs, thofe beauties to impart,
Which charm the foul, and meliorate the heart.

LINES

ADDRESSED TO THE

YOUNG LADIES

WHO ATTENDED

MR. CHILTON'S LECTURES

IN NATURAL PHILOSOPHY.

ANN. 1804—5.

The beafts, that roam o'er Lybia's defert plain,
Have gentler hearts than men who dare maintain
That woman, lovely woman, hath no foul,
They too feem drench'd in Circe's pois'nous bowl,
Who grant the fair may have a foul to fave,
But deem each female born an abject flave.
Give me the maiden of unfetterred mind,
By thought and knowledge ftrengthen'd and refin'd,

A gift like this more precious would I hold,
Than India's gems or Afric's pureſt gold.
Ye maids, whoſe vows to ſcience are addreſs'd,
If thus your minds be faſhion'd, thus impreſs'd,
With joy your courſe purſue, nor heed the while,
Envy's malignant grin, nor folly's ſmile ;
Trace nature's laws, explore the ſtarry maze ;
Learn why the lightnings flaſh, or meteors blaze,
From Earth to Heaven your view enquiring dart,
And ſee how order reigns in every part :
'Tis ſweet, 'tis wholeſome to frequent this ſchool,
Where all is beauty and unerring rule ;
But ſtrain'd reſearch becomes not well the fair,
Deep thought imparts a melancholy air,
The ſparkling eye grow s dim, the roſes fade
When long obſcur'd beneath the ſtudious ſhade :
Suffice it for a tender nymph to ſtray,
Where ſtrength and induſtry have clear'd the way,
To cull the fruits and flowers, which bleſs the toil,
Endur'd by Newton, Verulam, or Boyle.

Yet all possess not senses to enjoy
These flowers so fair, these fruits which never cloy.
There runs through all things that our powers can note
A golden thread that links the most remote,
There is a kindred feature to be trac'd,
In things most opposite, most widely plac'd ;
In matter thus, resemblance may be found,
To soaring mind, whose movements own no bound,
For as a fluid vainly strives to save
A heavier mass from sinking in its wave ;
So in the mind made up of trifles light,
All weighty truths, o'erwhelm'd, sink out of sight,
A while perchance, it may endure to feel
A sober thought's dread weight, as polish'd steel
Dropp'd gently on the water's face, seems loth
To sink, but 'tis repulsion holds them both.

Fair Science, how thy modest cheeks would glow,
If dragg'd to view, in fashion's puppet show,
'Midst fops and feathers, signs and painted cheeks,
Soft maiden blushes, and strange maiden freaks :

'Midſt ſickening pleaſures, weariſome delights,
Days doom'd to liſtneſsneſs, and ſleepleſs nights.
Ill would'ſt thou fare amidſt this gaudy train,
Where all is treacherous, tranſitory, vain !
No, no, the fair, who pant for joys like theſe,
Not wiſdom's richeſt ſtores of wealth could pleaſe,
Let Heaven and Earth, for them, be rul'd by chance,
No laws they heed, but thoſe which rule the dance ;
Their eyes faſt fix'd on earth, ne'er love to roam,
O'er all the ſplendors of the ſtarry dome,
For them, no ſtars o'er ſhone ſince time began,
With half the glories of a ſpangled fan.

To you, ye nymphs, inſpirers of my ſong,
No features here portray'd, I truſt, belong ;
But ſhould I ſee a girl at knowledge aim,
Becauſe Philoſophy's a handſome name,
Or who would learn becauſe the faſhion's ſo,
And beckon ſcience as ſhe would a beau,
This truth the trifler from my lips ſhould know :

" When nature fhall forget her 'ftablifh'd laws,
" And chance take place of an omnifcient caufe,
" When every creature fome ftrange powers fhall know,
" That cleaves the air, or treads the earth below,
" When bees, forgetful of their wonted fkill,
" Shall idly flaunt, while butterflies diftill
" The liquid fweets, or build the curious cell,
" Then may true wifdom grace a fluttering belle."

L.

LINES

ON COWPER THE POET,

WRITTEN AFTER READING THE LIFE OF HIM

BY HAYLEY.

Sweet melancholy Bard, whofe piercing thought,
Found humbleft themes with pure inftruction fraught,
How hard for mortal fight to trace the ways
Of Heav'n, throughout thy life's myfterious maze;
Why was it order'd that thy gentle mind,
Which fancy fired, and piety refined,
Should in this guilty world be forc'd to dwell,
Like fome bafe culprit in his gloomy cell,
Rous'd from its due repofe by feverifh dreams,
By goblin forms, by din of fancied fcreams?
Why was that fertile genius wafte and chill'd
By wintry blafts, its opening bloffoms kill'd?

A foil where Yemen's fpicy buds might blow,

And Perfia's rofe a purer fragrance know !

Why bloom'd fo late, thofe fweet poetic flowers,

Blefs'd by no fummer's funs, no vernal fhowers,

Which in the autumn of thy days were rear'd

By friendfhip's dew, by fickle zephirs cheer'd ?

I hear a diftant feraph bid me " hold,

" Nor tempt high heaven with enquiries bold,

" Weak fighted mortal, canft thou not difcern

" What from unaided reafon thou might'ft learn ?

" Had fortune's fun-beams cheer'd his early days,

" Amidft the foft favonian breath of praife,

" Thofe fruitful virtues, which fprung up fo fair,

" Thofe bloffoms breathing odours on the air,

" By weeds of pride and vanity o'ergrown,

" Unheeded might have bloom'd and died unknown.

" Prefumptuous mortal, 'twould become thee well,

" On this thy fellow mortal's life to dwell ;

" For in his breaft, when rack'd by fierceft woes,

" To queftion heav'n, no daring thought e'er rofe ;

" His actions vice and folly view with fhame,

" His precepts foul-mouth'd envy dares not blame,

" His well lov'd image ftill calls many a tear—

" His cherifh'd name all ages fhall revere.

L.

LINES

WRITTEN IN NOVEMBER, 1805.

The fiends of peſt, that from their dark wings ſhed
Infectious poiſon round, at length are fled :
Her ſtreaming flag Hygeia waves on high,
And ſoars triumphant in a cloudleſs ſky ;
She bids new fires the languid eye relume,
The faded cheek revive in freſher bloom :
She bids warm hope elate the fainting heart,
And pour the tide of life thro' every part.
Now crowding ſails the harbour fearleſs greet,
Sounds with loud hum the late deſerted ſtreet ;
A ſmile of joy, each brighten'd viſage wears,
Nor ſhews a ſingle trace of recent cares,

Nor thus with me : with anxious thought I turn
Where widows weep, and lonely orphans mourn ;
Still on my fancy dwell the fcenes of woe,
Whence gufh their tears, and lafting forrows flow.
He, whofe ftrong nerves were brac'd with health at night,
Feels the fwift peft, before returning light,
A morbid yellow fpread o'er all the fkin,
Declares the pangs that rage and wafte within :
Death rolls a burning tide thro' every vain,
And drives his phantoms 'crofs the wilder'd brain :
Th' affrighted neighbors fly the tainted ground,
And horrid filence reigns o'er all around ;
All aid is fruitlefs, vain is every care
And hope foon yields to uncontroll'd difpair.
E'er the fhrill fhriek proclaims he is no more,
Th' impatient hearfe already haunts the door :
In a rude cheft, the corfe yet warm, is plac'd,
The harden'd driver fpeeds with cruel hafte ;
In a loofe pit, the corfe yet warm, is thrown,
Deck'd with no turf, by no memorial known :

No rites are paid : no mournful train attends,
Nor o'er the grave, in pious anguifh bends——
Such are the fcenes that fix the wand'ring mufe,
And the heart bleeds at what the fancy views :

And tho' the fears, which late appall'd my breaft,
For thofe dear lives, in which my own is bleft,
Have ceas'd to act, a pious awe remains,
Which bows the foul, and o'er the fancy reigns,
Which turns, from fcenes of idle mirth, the view,
And gives to every thought, a folemn hue.

So when a ftorm collects, whofe gather'd gloom
Lightnings alone, with fitful flafh, illume :
If chance, half blinded by the tranfient blaze,
O'er the wide heath, a peafant, fearful, ftrays :
Tho' paft the ftorm, he reach his cot unharm'd,
Not yet fubfide the thoughts, that late alarm'd,
And while his children joyful crowd his chair,
He lifts to God, who fav'd, the folemn prayer.

N

VERSES

ADDRESSED TO A LADY,

Who maintained that there is more happiness in general at an advanced period of life, than in childhood.

Thy dimpled girls, and rosy boys
Rekindle in thy heart the joys,
   That bless'd thy tender years ;
Unheeded fleet the hours away ;
For while thy cherubs round thee play,
   New life thy bosom cheers.

Once more, thou tell'st me, I may taste,
E'er envious time this frame shall waste,
   My infant pleasures flown.
Ah ! there's a ray of lustre mild
Illumes the bosom of a child,
   To age, alas ! scarce known !

Not for my infant pleaſures paſt
I mourn : thoſe joys, which flew ſo faſt,
   They too had many a ſtain ;
But for the mind ſo pure and light,
Which made thoſe joys ſo fair, ſo bright,
   I ſigh, and ſigh in vain.

Well I remember you, bleſt hours !
Your ſun-beams bright, your tranſient ſhowers—
   Thoughtleſs I ſaw you fly ;
For diſtant ills then caus'd no dread,
Nor car'd I for the moments fled,
   For mem'ry call'd no ſigh.

My parents dear then rul'd each thought,
No blame I fear'd, no praiſe I ſought,
   But what their love beſtow'd :
Full ſoon I learnt each meaning look,
Nor e'er the angry glance miſtook,
   For that where rapture glow'd.

'Twas then when evening call'd to reft,
I'd feek a father to requeft
   His benediction mild :
A Mother's love more loud would fpeak,
With kifs on kifs fhe'd print my cheek,
   And blefs her darling child.

Thy lighteft mifts, and clouds, fweet Sleep !
Thy pureft opiates, thou doft keep,
   On infancy to fhed ;
No guilt there checks thy foft embrace,
And not e'en tears and fobs can chafe
   Thee from an infant's bed.

The trickling tears which flow'd at night,
Oft haft thou ftay'd, 'till morning light
   Difpell'd my little woes ;
So fly before the fun-beams pow'r
 The remnants of the evening fhow'r,
   Which wet the early rofe.

Farewell bleft hours ! full faft ye flew,
And that, which made your blifs fo true,
   Ye would not leave behind ;
The glow of youth ye could not leave,
But why, why cruelly bereave
   Me of my artlefs mind ?

The fair unwrinkl'd front of youth,
The vermeil cheek, the fmile of truth,
   Deep lines of care foon mark ;
But can no power preferve the foul,
Unwarp'd by pleafure's foft controul,
   Uumov'd by paffions dark ?

Thefe changes which o'ertake our frame,
Alas ! are emblems of the fame ,
   Which on our foul attend ;
Yet who reviews the courfe he's run
But thinks where life once more begun,
   Unfpotted it fhould end.

Vain thought ! the evening's firm resolve
We break ere morning clouds dissolve,
 Then boast the life we'd led,
Would heav'n but infancy restore :
Thus o'er an idle dream we pore,
 But slight the waking deed.

Fond Mother ! hope thy bosom warms,
That on the prattler in thy arms,
 Heav'n's choicest gifts will flow :
Thus let thy prayer incessant rise,
Content, if he who rules the skies,
 But half the boon bestow.

" O thou, whose view is ne'er estrang'd
" From innocence, preserve unchang'd
 " Through life my darling's mind ;
" Unchang'd its truth and purity,
" Still fearless of futurity,
 " Still artless, though refin'd.

ADDRESSED TO A LADY.

" As oft his anxious nurfe has caught
" And fav'd his little hand, that fought
  " The bright, but treach'rous blaze :
" So may fair wifdom keep him fure
" From glitt'ring vices which allure
  " Through life's delufive maze.

" Oh may the ills, which man surround,
" Like paffing fhadows on the ground,
  " Obfcure, not ftain my boy !
" Then may he gently drop to reft,
" Calm as a child by fleep oppreft,
  " And wake to endlefs joy.

L.

LINES TO PETROSA.

Thy charms, Petrofa, which infpire
Unnnmber'd fwains to chant thy praife,
Bid me too join the tuneful choir,
My faint and tim'rous voice to raife.

And though more lofty fongs invite,
Regard, for once, an humble fwain,
The warbling thrufh can oft delight,
More than the fkylark's louder ftrain.

Thy heav'nly form, thy virtues too,
In notes of praife afcend the fkies;
To opening charms, which ftrike the view,
Unceafing afpirations rife.

But midſt theſe charms by all confeſt,
One fault thy hopeleſs ſwains declare ;
A heart there dwells within that breaſt,
Which knows no love, which heeds no prayer.

Deſpondent ſighs, and notes of pain
Delight, they ſay, Petroſa's ear :
To ſue for pity were as vain,
As from the rocks to ask a tear.

Oh ſenſeleſs throng ! that callous breaſt
Proclaims her nature's favor'd child
While others pine, with love oppreſt,
Her thoughts are free, her ſlumbers mild.

And all that ſoftneſs which gives grace,
And honor to the female heart,
Though diſtant from its wonted place,
She harbors in a nobler part.

For though that heart to every found,
Which would compaſſion move, be dull,
The foftnefs, which ſhould there be found,
Kind nature granted to her.......skull.

                        L.

A SONG.

No more glows the weſt, with the ſun's parting beams,
The ſhadows of even deſcend o'er the ſcene,
The moon, her mild light, thro' the blue heaven ſtreams,
And the ſilver rays tremble the branches between.

'Tis here in this ſilent receſs of the grove,
Where the ſtreamlet's ſoft voice alone meets the ear;
'Tis here that I wait, anxious wait, for my love—
And the leaves' gentle ruſtle gives hoe p ſhe is near.

I ſee, thro' the tall trees, her fairy form glide,
A white flowing robe lightly veils o'er her charms,
While my eyes ſtill purſue her, ſhe darts to my ſide—
With quick tranſport I riſe, and am preſt in her arms.

The vows, that fo often have pafs'd, I renew,
She hears, fhe approves, with a fweet trufting fmile,
And curft be the wretch, who, that fweet fmile, could view,
And a thought entert in of deception or guile.

I fwear by the light, which now foftens the grove,
That light fo propitious ! to lovers fo dear !
I would fooner lofe life, than lofe Anna's love—
I would fooner lofe life, than caufe Anna a tear.

ANACREON,

ODE 37,

BARNES' EDITION.

See Spring advance, with lightfome pace,
Joyful mien, and blufhing face !
Mark the Graces, in her train,
Scattering rofes o'er the plain !
As in his troubled ftream they lave,
See old Ocean fmooth his wave !
The bird that fled from winter's fight,
Returning fpeds his homeward flight ;
The darken'd fun repairs his beams,
And now in all his fplendor flames.

O

No longer ftorms deface the year ;
  Again the ruftic's toils appear ;
Frefh-fpringing flowers deck the vale,
  And breathe a rich and fragrant gale ;
  With leafy honors crown'd once more,
The olive guards his rip'ning ftore ;
  The gadding vine o'erfpreads the ground,
And weaves his flexile arms around ;
The grape, with purple juice, 'gins fwell,
The juice, whofe joys I love to tell.

IMITATION.

AMERICAN SPRING.

===

See Spring advance, with changeful face,
Diforder'd mien, and trembling pace !
Now on the turf fhe loves to reft,
And deck with op'ning flow'rs her breaft ;
She moves, and verdure fpreads the ground,
She fmiles, and nature fmiles around :

But foon dark frowns her face deform,
She calls again the winter-ftorm ;
He drives his blafts acrofs the fcene,
And withers all its rifing green.

Now reigns the Sun, in perfect day,
And Earth, exulting, owns his fway;
And now, involv'd in clouds, retires,
And burns with ineffectual fires.

The fearful ruftic feeks his field,
Which hope fcarce tells, what crop fhall yield,
With anxious look, regards the fky,
And hardly dares his labor ply.

The trees, fcarce ftrew'd with leaves, appear,
And feem the coming blaft to fear :
No poet chaunts his " wood notes wild,"
Nor haunts the grove " rapt fancy's child."

Yet Spring, tho' changeful be thy face,
In every change thou haft a grace,
A grace, that in my partial eyes,
Excels the charm of Afian fkies.

ANACREON,

ODE 39,

BARNES' EDITION.

When I quaff rich generous wine,
I feel, at once, a glow divine ;
Poſſeſs'd with all the muſe's fire,
Strike, with rapid hand, the lyre.

When I quaff the mantling bowl,
Care and grief deſert the ſoul,
All anxious thoughts are put to flight,
As clouds before the morning light.

When the mantling bowl I quaff,
Jolly Bacchus prompts the laugh,
Rolls me o'er midſt fragrant flowers,
And ſteeps in mirth the careleſs hours.

When I quaff rich generous wine,
A chaplet round my brows I twine
And fing to each enraptur'd gueft,
The pleafures of a life of reft.

When I quaff the mantling bowl,
The God of love invades my foul ;
I feel, I feel the fair one's charms,
And lofe my fenfes in her arms.

When in cups of ample fize,
The fparkling juice attracts my eyes,
I joy, where youth and wit invite,
To pafs in focial mirth the night.

Remote from care and public ftrife,
Thefe are the joys, which fweeten life:
Thefe bleffings to my fhare ftill fall,
Tho' death may come, who comes to all.

TRANSLATION

OF ONE OF THE CHORUSES

IN THE

PROMETHEUS OF ÆSCHYLUS

———

Prometheus is reprefented as chained to a rock, by the command of Jupiter for having conveyed fire from heaven and taught the ufe of it to men : for having alfo inftructed them in many ufeful arts, of which it had been decreed that they fhould remain ignorant. The chorus is compofed of Sea-Nymphs, who addrefs him as follows :

Oh may no thought of mine e'er move,
The vengeance of almighty Jove !
Ne'er fhall my incenfe ceafe to rife,
Due to the powers who rule the fkies,

From all the watery domains,
O'er which my father Ocean reigns:
And till his towery billows ceafe
To roll, lull'd in eternal peace,
Ne'er fhall an impious word of mine,
Irreverence mark to power divine.

Lightly flew my former days,
With not a cloud to dim the rays
Of hope, which promis'd peace to fend,
And golden pleafures without end.
But what a blaft now mars my blifs,
Prometheus, at a fcene like this.
While thus thy tortures I behold,
I fhudder at the thoughts fo bold,
Which could impel thee to withftand
For mortal man, Jove's dread command.

Where now the aid from mortals due
For all thy deeds of love fo true?

TRANSLATION.

Alas ! their fhadowy ftrength is vain,
As dreams which haunt the fever'd brain ;
Ah ! how fhould fleeting fhades like thefe
Refift almighty Jove's decrees ?

Such thoughts will rife, fuch ftrains will flow
Prometheus, at thy bitter woe.
How different was the ftrain I fang,
When round thy bridal chamber rang
The voices of the choral throng,
Who pour'd the hymeneal fong
To thee, and to thy joy, thy pride,
Hefione, thy blooming bride.

                                        L.

WAR SONG,

FROM THE GREEK OF

TYRTÆUS.

Habemus etiam Tyrtæi illius reliquas, qui
     " mares animos in martia bella
" Verfibus exacuit."

Omnes, de bellicâ fortitudine, de patriæ amore, de immortali gloriâ virorum in acie ftrenué occumbentium, quæ timidis etiam audaciam addere poffent ; quibus Lacædæmonios debititatos jamdudum fractosque animo, ad certam fpem victoriæ erexit.

        LOWTH, de Sac. Poe. Heb. Prælec 1, p. 16.

Spartans, roufe, your country calls,
    Children, Wives, your aid demand ;
Curft the wretch, whom fear appals,
    Save, oh ! fave your native land.

With foul-fraught ardor, feek the fight,
And fhed your blood, with proud delight,
Prefs forward, in compacted band,
And death prefer to fhameful flight.
　Each advancing choofe his foe,
　　* Fix the teeth, and knit the brow,
　Strain the finews, fwell the breaft,
　Shake horror from the lofty creft ;
　With ftrong right hand, the faulchion wield,
　Set foot to foot, and fhield to fhield ;

　　* *Stiffen the finews, fummon up the blood—*
　Now fet the teeth, and ftretch the noftrils wide,
　Hold hard the breath and bend up every fpirit
　To his full height.
　　　　　　　　HEN. 5. A. 2, s. 2.

　Before the publication of Dr. Farmer's Effay, this coincidence might have been adduced with fome plaufibility, as a proof of Shakefpeare's knowledge and imitation of the ancients—It does indeed prove that both poets obferved nature with equal accuracy.

As the foe approaches near,
Wrench his fword, or weighty fpear,
In mighty grafp, entwine him round,
And hurl him, ftruggling, to the ground.
Know, that the man, whofe facred fword
Is drawn to guard his native land,
Tho' forc'd from light, by Mars abhorr'd,
To wander o'er the Stygian ftrand,
Does not die ; tho' earth receive
His corfe, his glory ftill fhall live ;
Tho' ftretch'd, and dull, and cold he lie,
He triumphs ftill, and DOES NOT DIE.

ODE

FROM THE SPANISH OF GARCILASO DE LA VEGA

How bleft is he, who free from care
Inhales the country's wholefome air,
   'Midft folitude and fhade ;
Who from his breaft each anxious thought
Drives far away, nor harbors aught,
   That can his peace invade.

The haughty threfholds of the great,
Their crowded halls, and lordly ftate
   No longer he frequents ;
Nor on the falfe and flattering race,
Who hunger after power or place,
   His indignation vents.

P

He's now no more oblig'd to feign,
To aſk, to tremble, or complain,
    As ſuits the changing hour ;
But free in thought, in word, and deed,
Directs his ſteps as chance may lead,
    And dreads no lordling's power.

Thoſe objects, that are wont inſpire
So many breaſts with wild deſire,
    He views with calm diſdain :
Careleſs alike of wealth and place,
He ſcorns to join the ſordid race,
    A worthleſs prize to gain.

Beneath the oak or cheſnut's ſhade,
Whoſe branches canopy the glade,
    In muſing wrapt he lies ;
Or marks the quiet herds that rove
Wide ſcatter'd thro' the neighb'ring grove,
    And feaſts his roving eyes.

ODE FROM THE SPANISH.

Thro' pebbly channels limpid flows
A stream, which soothing to repose,
  In murmurs glides along.
While birds who own no master's sway,
Warble their sweet, tho' untaught lay,
  And pour the varied song.

With busy hum the bee now plies
From tender flower to flower, and flies
  With fragrant load opprest—
While all that can compose the mind,
The rustling leaves, the whisp'ring wind,
  Invite the soul to rest.

N.

TRANSLATIONS FROM TASSO.

The following tranflations from the " Jerufalem Delivered," afpire to little more than the praife of faithful, and indeed almoft literal interpretation, if upon comparifon, they fhould be found to convey a jufter reprefentation of the original, than the correfponding paffages of Mr. Hoole's Verfion, the fuperiority muft be afcribed to the peculiar fitnefs of blank verfe, as the medium of tranflation, where the original is fo remarkably diftinguifhed by energy, majefty, and fimplicity of ftyle ; qualities, which, it cannot be denied, are more eafily attained or preferved in blank verfe, than in rhyme. It muft, in a great meafure, be owing to his choice of the latter, that Mr. Hoole is moft deficient in thofe particulars, in which Taffo chiefly excels.* The fubject naturally fuggefts a remark,

* *It may be objected that Taffo himfelf made choice of rhyme ; but it should be recollected, that the Italian octave ftanza is fufceptible of nearly as much eafe and variety as blank verfe.*

which modern readers and writers of poetry ſhould bear perpetually in mind; it is, that Homer, Taſſo, and Milton, the moſt ſublime and impreſſive of poets, are at the ſame time the moſt ſimple in their ſtyle, and the moſt ſparing in the uſe of epithets.

———

God ſends Gabriel to the city of Tortoſa to command Godfrey to aſſemble and rouſe to action the Chriſtian leaders, and to inform him of his appointment to the chief command.

GER. LIB. CAN. I, ST. 13—15.

Thus ſpake th' Omnipotent ; and Gabriel ſtraight
Prepar'd to execute his dread beheſt.
His angel form inviſible, with air
He cloath'd, and to the ſight obtuſe of man
Subjecting, feign'd a human ſhape and face,
Which ſtill celeſtial majeſty retain'd.
He ſeems, not yet a youth, nor ſtill a child,

P 2

And round his locks, a radiant glory plays ;
His wings, of pureft white, are tipt with gold,
Upborne on thefe, in fwifteft flight, he parts
The wind and cloud ; on these, fublime, he foars
O'er earth and fea, unconfcious of fatigue.
When thus array'd, the herald of the fkies,
Towards this low earth, obedient, bent his way ;
O'er mount Libanus firft, his rapid courfe,
On equal balanc'd wings upheld, he check'd ;
Then down directed to Tortofa's plain
His flight precipitate.   The glorious fun,
Now juft emerging from the eaftern coaft,
Was ftill, in part, beneath the waves conceal'd,
And Godfrey, as his pious ufe requir'd,
Addrefs'd his orifons to heav'n, when lo !
From th' eaftern fky, and with the rifing fun,
Tho' brighter far, the meffenger of Heav'n
Appear'd, and thus the chriftian chief befpake.

N.

Armida having endeavoured, in vain, to prevent the departure of Rinaldo from the enchanted Ifland, vents her indignation in the moſt paſſionate exclamations and returns to her palace vowing revenge on her faith-lefs lover.

Impetuous thus, with interrupted voice,
She raves, as from the folitary ſhore
She turns her ſteps.   Her wild diſhevell'd locks,
Her rolling eyes, and face with rage inflam'd,
Declare the furies that poſſeſs her breaſt.
Now to her palace come, with direful voice,
Three hundred helliſh fpirits ſhe invokes ;
The fun grows pale ; dark clouds involve the ſky,
And ruſhing whirlwinds ſhake the mountain tops ;
Lo ! from beneath infernal founds proceed,
And, frequent, thro' the ample halls are heard,
Hiſſes, and howls, and ſhrieks, and fearful yells ;
O'er all a more than midnight darkneſs broods,
Thro' which no mingl'ing ray is feen, fave when
The light'ning's flaſh gleams thro' th' obfcure profound ;

The fhades at length difpers'd, again the fun,
While noxious vapours ftill opprefs the air,
Reftores his pale, and yet uncertain light :
No palace now appears, not e'en a trace,
To mark the fpot where late it ftood, remains.
As when in clouds fantaftic forms are feen,
And air-built piles of fhort endurance,
Which the wind difperfes, or the fun diffolves,
Or as the fancies of a fick man's brain,
So vanifh'd quite the palace ; nought remains,
But alpine rocks, in native horrors clad.

Ger. Lib. Can. 16, S. 68, 71.

N.

Ifmeno, the Pagan Sorcerer, to deprive the Christians of all means of repairing their warlike engines, enchants the wood which had fupplied them with timber, and from which alone it could be procured.

In a lone valley, from the chriftian tents
Not far remov'd, afcends a lofty wood,
Whofe clofe-rang'd trees, in ancient rudenefs wild,
O'er all around diffufe a fearful fhade.
Here, when the noontide fun fhines brighteft, dwells
A fad, uncertain, glooming light* ; like that
Which doubtful breaks thro' fkies by clouds obfcur'd,
When day to night fucceeds, or night to day ;
But when the fun withdraws his beams, here foon
Prevail impenetrable gloom, and night,
And horrors like th' infernal, which the fenfe
Opprefs with blindnefs, and appal the foul.
Hither no fhepherd e'er, no herdfman guides

* " *A little glooming light much like a shade* "
                Spencer, Fairy Queen, Can. 11.

His flocks his herds or food or fhade to feek.
No trav'ller here, fave when bewilder'd, treads ;
But feeks a diftant path, and marks with awe.
Hither, by night, the witching hags, in crowds,
Each by her paramour attended, come ;
They come by clouds upborne, this under fhape
Of hideous ferpent, this of goat deform'd.
Shamelefs affembly ! which the fhadow vain
Of fancied good, thus ufes to allure,
With filthy fhow, and vile, to celebrate
Its impious nuptial rites, and feafts profane.
Thus ftood belief ; and none that dwelt around
This dreaded wood, had ever torn a branch ;
Its facred fhades the Franks (for hence alone
Might they their engines rear,) firft dar'd invade.
Hither, of night the filence deep and apt
Awaiting, came Ismeno, on the night
Next that on which the tow'r, that threat'ning hung
O'er Sion's walls, in flaming ruin fell,

And trac'd his circle, and the figns imprefs'd.
And now ungirt, with one foot bare, receiv'd
Within the round, he mutter'd forceful fpells ;
Thrice to the Eaft his face he turn'd, and thrice
Survey'd the realms, where finks the fetting fun ;
And thrice that wand he fhook, with which the dead
Evoking from their tombs, he oft compels
To live and move again ; with naked foot
Thrice ftruck the ground ; then fhouting loud exclaim'd,
" Hear, hear, O ye, who from the ftarry fphere,
" By founding li htnings, were precipitate
" Hurl'd down ; as well, ye, who the ftorm excite,
" And tempeft, wand'ring habitants of air ;
" As ye, who minifter to finful fouls
" The caufe of endlefs woe, inhabitants
" Of Erebus, I here invoke your aid ;
" And thine, dread King of Hades' flaming bounds ;
" Take in ftrict charge this foreft, and thefe trees,
" Which, number'd, to your care I now confign,

" As to the foul, the body both abode

" Supplies, and vefture, fo fhall unto you

" Thefe trunks, that thus the Franks far hence may flee,

" At leaft the axe withhold, and dread your rage."

He faid; and words fo horrible fubjoin'd,

As none but impious tongue may dare repeat;

At which the lights adorning the ferene

Of night fhine dimly; and the troubled moon,

Her horns in clouds involving, difappears.

He then, enrag'd, with fhouts redoubled, cries:

" Invoked fpirits, do ye ftill refufe

" Your prefence? whence this long delay? perhaps,

" Sounds yet more potent, more occult, ye wait?

" Nor have I yet forgotten, thro' difufe,

" The fureft method of the direful art;

" Still do I know, from mouth with blood defil'd,

" To fpeak that great, that dreaded name, at which

" Hell dares not deaf or obftinate remain;

" Nor Pluto's felf be carelefs to obey.

" What thus? what thus?" Yet more he would have faid,
But ftraight he knew the charm comp etely form'd.
* Unnumber'd fpirits came and countlefs; fome,
Who wand'ring dwelt amid the fields of air,
And fome, forth iffuing from the gloomy caves
Profound of earth, with tardy motion came;
The high decree yet dreading, which their ufe
Of armed fight forbad; but thus to come,
Did not prevent, nor in thefe trees to dwell.

GER. LIB. CAN. 13.   s. 2—11.

N.

* *Innumerabili infiniti. Several inftances of the adoption
of this Italian idiom, if I am not greatly miftaken, are
to be found in Milton tho' I cannot readily turn to the
paffages.*   Ed.

SONNET

FROM PETRARCH—I

Zefiro torna, e'l bel tempo rimena, &c.

Now Spring returns, and leads her smiling train,
  And spreads, o'er hill and vale, the living green;
  Again with music, wakes the woodland scene,
And decks with flowers, of varied hue, the plain ;
The winds are hush'd, and peace broods o'er the main,
  The meadows laugh beneath the blue serene,
  O'er earth, air, sea, the power of love is seen,
And thrills through all that lives the pleasing pain:
  But not to me the genial spring restores
  The joys, her presence erst was wont inspire,
  But wakes, to anguish wakes, the sense of woe :

In vain, her charms on all around fhe pours,
Thee, Laura, ftill thefe cheerlefs eyes require,
And reft of thee, no gleam of pleafure know.

This exquifite fonnet has been imitated, and perhaps equalled, by Drummond of Hawthornden, (part.
2, fon 7.) inde.d all the fonnets of that admirable,
though neglected poet, are truly Petrarchian, and un-
doubtedly the moft perfect which our language can
boaft. If we believe Mr. Good, the learned and poetical tranflator of Lucretius, Petrarch is himfelf an
imitator. (Good's Lucretius, v. 1, p. 13.)

ANOTHER FROM THE SAME.—II.

Pommi, ove'l fol occide i fiori e l'erba, &c.

———

Yes ! place me, where the fun, with blafting ray,
Kills every herb ; or where perpetual cold
Has fix'd the feas, in icy mountains roll'd ;
Or mid bleft climes, that boaft the temper'd day,
And perfect year, exalt to wealth and fway ;
    Or let proud fortune every gift withold ;
    * Let Death, with damp and murky wing infold ;
Or thro' each vein life's rapid current ftray ;

* ———   ———   ——— *Seu Mors atris circumvolat alis.*
                    Hor. B 2, Sat. 1, L. 58.

Or Death's black wing already be difplay'd,
To wrap me in the univerfal shade :   Pope.

Whether Oblivion ſhroud, or Fame reſound,
In heaven, on earth, or in th' abyſs profound,
Such as I was, ſtill ſuch ſhall I be found;
Still will I pour the deep, the heartfelt ſtrain,
Still o'er my breaſt ſhall Love, and Laura reign,
The ſource of all my bliſs, and all my pain.

The idea of this ſonnet was evidently ſuggeſted by
the celebrated ſtanzas, with which Horace concludes
the twenty-ſecond ode of his firſt book.
Pone me, pigris ubi nulla campis &c.
Drummond furniſhes another ſucceſsful imitation.
(Part 1. Son. 69.)

TO MISS ——————. III.

Tho' love be faid to have infpiring force,
    And e'en in untaught breafts to wake the mufe,
    That neither thoughts, nor words, doth then refufe,
But gives to flow of tender verfe the courfe :
Yet in my faithful breaft, tho' long the fource
    Of love, fervent and pure, as e'er could boaft,
    The moft enraptur'd of Apollo's hoft,
Ne'er can the " cruel boy," this law enforce.
    Ah ! wonder not, tho' apt on other themes,
The mufe fhould here be mute ; to fpeak my love,
    Thy merits to exprefs, a tafk fhe deems,
Which to attempt, would folly only prove—
    Not Maro's felf could hope, in equal verfe,
    Thy virtues, grace, and beauty, to rehearfe.

TO THE SAME.—IV.

O thou most cherish'd in my secret heart,
   With purest zeal enshrin'd, and worshipp'd there,
Still, still I see, as when compell'd to part,
   Thy trembling form—the wildly pensive air
With which thou bad'st adieu—the big drops start,
   And course thy pallid cheek—thou breath'st a pray'r,
That he, who reigns above, will deign impart
   His grace divine, and save us from despair.
What were my feelings then?—to madness wrought,
   Now, in convulsive glee, I laugh aloud—
Now, fix'd as marble, stand entranc'd in thought,
   While woe's dark visions on my fancy crowd;
Till rous'd at length, " I cannot, must not stay"—
Prest thy cold lips again, and rush'd away.

V.

" His virtues form'd the magic of his song."

* * * * * * * * *

———

Cowper, affertor of the moral fong,
    Thou England's glory, in degenerate days,
    And juft inheritor of ancient praife,
How fhall I fpeak thy worth, nor do thee wrong ?
Unforc'd by art, in native vigor ftrong,
    Thy pure, and fimple, and pathetic lays,
    Replete with thought, and bright with fancy's rays,
Proclaim thee firft amid the tuneful throng ;
Yes ! in thy verfe a fecret charm we find,
    A charm not taught, and ne'er attain'd by art,
At once it gratifies, and fills the mind,
    And foftens, wakes, and meliorates the heart.
'Tis that we trace thy mind, and virtues here,
And that we know, and feel thee ftill fincere.

VI.

O Burns ! when I perufe thy nervous page,
  Where, fcenes adorn'd by genius' brighteft hues,
  And pathos' fofteft tints, the fpirit views,
Feelings, at once of mingled fcorn and rage,
Will rife, againft the proud and felfifh age,
  That wonder'd at thy wild unletter'd mufe,
  And while it prais'd, yet, niggard, could refufe
The proper meed ; nor rais'd thee to the ftage,
Where God and nature deftin'd thee to ftand ;
  Whence had we feen thy genius all difplay'd,
And ftreaming fplendor o'er thy native land,
  All thy bright foul, in warm effulgence ray'd ;
But left thee on bleak poverty's dark ftrand,
  Where fweeps the furge, and chilling blafts invade.

TO WILLIAM COBBETT, ESQ.

EDITOR OF THE POLITICAL REGISTER—VII.

———

Cobbett ! altho' thy blind or envious foes
    With base attempt, impeach thy honeft fame,
    And brand thee with each foul opprobrious name,
Still perfevere ; with fearlefs pen expofe
The " bold bad men" who caufe thy country's woes ;
    Still perfevere, with fix'd and conftant aim,
    Till every breaft fhall feel the patriot flame,
Whence England's proud and ancient glories rofe.
Should thofe black clouds at length be over-blown,
    Which menace ruin to thy native land,
The day muft come, when ALL thy worth fhall own,
    And give the praife, thy zeal and cares demand,

When Factions felf no longer d are accufe,
And thou fhalt gain a wreath from every Mufe.

Notwithftanding the prejudices which prevail fo extenfively in this country, I difdain to make any apology for the above Sonnet.   I own, I cannot help feeling an intereft in the fate of England ;   and I am firmly perfuaded, that no man, of common fenfe or candor, can perufe with attention the writings of Mr. Cobbett, and not be convinced both of the integrity of his motives, and the importance of his exertions.

VIII.

I, late escap'd the city's noisome air,
   The din of commerce and the busy throng
   Who seek for wealth, by methods right or wrong,
And waste their lives in toil, their souls with care,
With joy, to nature's artless scenes repair;
   Unspent in breath, in new-born vigour strong,
   O'er rocks, and rushing streams I bound along,
And e'en the mountain's highest summit dare;
Awhile I pause to catch a fresher gale,
   Then to some distant field I dart away,
Plunge in the wood, the grove, or shaded vale,
   And lost in wild uncertain rapture stray:
I feel my thoughts to nobler heights aspire,
   And strike, with bolder hand, the sounding lyre.

IX.

How fweet to draw the fragrant breath of morn ;
 To mark the fun's large orb majeftic rife,
 While rapid ftreams of light o'erfpread the fkies,
* And fleecy clouds in thoufand hues adorn !
How fweet in fome romantic glen, that lies
 Beyond the rage of noon, where ftreamlets, borne
 Down broken channels in the rough rock worn,
Roll murmuring on, to reft and clofe the eyes !
How fweet, at eve, to climb the mountains height,
 To fee o'er plains below the fhade extend,
And watch the progrefs of departing light,
 At length, with flow and mufing ftep defcend,
And reach our cot, as falls a darker night ;
 There meet the charms, which love and friendfhip blend.

* *The clouds in thoufand liveries dight.*
L'ALLEGRO.

R

TRANSLATION OF COWPER'S VOTUM.

Cowper's Poems, v. 1, p. 284.

Ye dews of morn ! ye breezes wafting health !
Ye groves and green banks of the murmuring ftream !
Ye turf-crown'd hills ! ye vales of cool recefs !
The fimple pleafures, that I once enjoy'd,
In my paternal fields, remote from art,
From fear remote, would but the fates reftore :
The world unknowing, to the world unknown,
How gladly would I fpend my future days,
And wait ferene and calm th' approach of age ;
And when my years, years not unbleft, have clof'd,
And death, with gentle fweep, has láid me low,
O may the fwelling turf, or filent ftone
Alone denote where I fecurely lie.

IMITATION

OF SOME STANZAS

FROM THE

AMBRA OF LORENZO DE MEDICI.

O mifer chi tra l'onde trova fuora, &c.

Unhappy he, who wand'ring far from fhore,
  Amid the ocean's wafte, where night has fpread
Her thickeft glooms around, and tempefts pour,
  And wreck their fury on his fencelefs head,
Expects the day, and ftill by hope mifled,
  Fancies the fhades of darknef, 'gin retire ;
Fancies he views the ftreaks of paler red,
  Which fpeak th' approach of the eternal fire,
That ftill far 'neath the waves, his brilliance doth attire.

How different is the happy lovers' lot,
   Ne'er point their wifhes to the coming day ;
All griefs difmiffed and anxious cares forgot,
   Their thoughts tend folely to their amorous play ;
To them obfcure and tedious i the day,
   And the fun lingers to conceal his beams ;
But night, with lightning-fwiftnefs, fpeeds her way ;
   And oh ! far fhorter than the day it feems,
And fcarce it feems begun, when morning twilight gleams.

*STANZAS

OF A POEM

ENTITLED THE

TRIUMPH OF WOMAN.

——

CONTENTS.

Invocation—fecret affembly of the ladies—characters and fpeeches of feveral of the members   Euphelia rifes—dominion of man not founded on the advantages of his corporeal frame ; many animals fuperior to him in ftrength, fwiftnefs, &c. yet all have been tam'd to his ufe or dread his power ; nor on any natural fuperiority of his mental faculties ; but folely on the igno-

*There is a confiderable hiatus in the manufcript of this poem ; fhould the pub.ic add " . alde deflendus" it may p offibly be fupplied.

rance in which woman is defignedly kept—knowledge
is power—neceffity of the cultivation of the mind—
prediction of the confequences which will refult from
fuch cultivation—applaufe and refolutions of the affembly—engagement of Mr. Chilton, &c.—wonderful
progrefs of the ladies in every branch of fcience—
alarm and terror of the beaux—conclufion.

O were I fkill'd in necromantic lore,
   *And could employ the might of magic fpell,
Forth from his lowly bed, Dan Spencer hoar,
   With rite of forcefull fway, would I compel ;
In reverent accents pray the fhade to tell,
   Whence flow the charms that ftill entrance the mind,
And give his fong all others to excel ;
   Ah who thy lay infpir'd, what fairy kind,
All thy verfes fmooth'd, and every thought refin'd.

* — — — — — — — — O who can tell
The hidden power of herbs, and might of magic fpell.
             Spencer, F. Q. b. v, c. ii.

The folemn epic trump like thee to found,
　And roufe the giant War with mighty blaft,
While Horror, Rage, and Danger crowd around,
　And Terror wildly glares, " in trance aghaft ;"
Of ancient deeds to tell and ages paft,
　When lordly Chivalry maintain'd his fway,
And each true knight, in burnifh'd mail yclafpt,
　Rufh'd ardent forth, his fummons to obey,
While glory from their helms his brighteft beams did ray;

I dare not afk ; this envied height to tow'r,
　And foar undazzled to the folar flame,
Is thine alone ; may " bale and bitter ftowre"
　Purfue the wight, that would impeach thy fame ;
Enough, O courteous fhade, to gild my name,
　Thy leffer praifes fhould'ft thou chufe impart,
The harmony, that Murder's felf might tame,
　The fimple graces that emove the heart,
And happy negligence, that feems to fcorn all art.

Where Hudfon proud his mighty ftream outpours,
   And fwells the ocean with his copious tide,
A fpacious city on his margin foars,
   Of weftern realm the glory and the pride;
What ftore of beauteous damfels here abide,
   Who Love's fweet reign o'er every heart extend,
And fpread his triumphs round on every fide,
   How fhall my verfe compute? or whom commend,
When for the golden prize, fo many fair contend?

Not the fam'd rofes that in England blow,
   Can boaft the vermeil tints and foften'd flufh,
That on thefe Damfels' cheeks are wont to glow;
   Not fuch the luftre of Aurora's blufh,
If from the heart the lucid currénts rufh,
   Impell'd by anger or ingenuous fhame;
The " foft embodied" fays, that fcarcely crufh
   The waving grafs, whiles to the moon's pale flame,
Their feftive fports they hold, and rings myfterious frame;

TRIUMPH OF WOMAN.

Not with such grace, such airy lightness fleet,
  As when these Damsels, in the mazy dance,
Deceive the eye, with " many twinkling" feet ;
  Who can resist that soft, that seraph glance,
That takes the ravish'd soul, in pleasing trance,
  And opes the joys of Eden on the mind ?
Let Fable now be silent, and Romance,
  Not spells like this amid their tales we find,
That thus subdue the soul, and all the senses bind.

The visions that enchant the poet's eye,
  When youth is ardent, and when Fancy sways,
Tho' bright with colours of celestial dye,
  Tho' deck'd with inspiration's purest rays,
Yet ne'er such transports of devotion raise ;
  Ne'er to such height of rapture lift the soul,
Nor match the charms, that here assembled blaze ;
  I feel their influence now my breast controul,
And bid the stream of verse, its tide resistless roll.

Yet not thefe charms of perifhable grace,
   Whofe fragrance and whofe bloom fo foon decay ;
Not charms that Time hath licence to efface,
   Should prompt, alone, my tributary lay ;
If not illum'd by that furpaffing ray,
   Which virtue poureth from her inward fhrine,
My lyre, to found their praife, fhould not affay ;
   But here with beauty mental graces join,
And all the virtues bright with mingled luftre fhine.

Nor this their higheft praife ; but thoughts elate,
   Which fcorn fubjection, and to rule afpire :
Which fcorn their fex's too dependant ftate,
   And plans of innovation bold infpire ;
The love of fame, and freedom's holy fire
   Here glow unquench'd in every female breaft :
Difdain of haughty Man, and generous ire,
   On every female vifage, ftand confeft,
And frowns and threatning clouds each female brow inveft.

Ah ! lovely woman, how fevere thy fate !
  How joys the tyrant Man to caufe thy woe !
How many ways he feeks to gain thy hate,
  And force the bitter tears of forrow flow !
Well may thy cheek with indignation glow,
  And well thine eye, its angry lightning flafh ;
But now a fpeedy fall awaits thy foe,
  Whom foon thy virtue from the height fhall dafh
Of all his pride, and wide fhall fpread the fatal crafh.

In all the regions of the varied globe,
  (Where flames the fun, with unremitting ray,
And nature wears unchang'd her fummer robe ;
  Or where his beams fcarce dart the lingering day,
And on th' impaffive ice the light'nings play)
  Woman the flave, ftill Man the lord we find ;
In camp and fenate ftill he bears the fway,
  While fhe (the privilege of thought refign'd)
To low delights, and mean domeftic cares is ftill confin'd.

But foon the Tyrant, in his turn, fhall mourn,
    And bow his haughty neck to woman's rule,
While laurel wreaths her polifh'd brow adorn.
    Tho' waters n antling in the ftagnant pool,
Nor cheer the fields, the fcorching air nor cool,
    Yet, if releaf'd they fpread their ftreams around,
(A fimile you'll fay of Homer's fchool)
    With waving plenty laughs the teeming ground,
And fongs of grateful joy thro' all the vale refound,

And thus, when Woman fhall commence her reign,
    Shall joyful earth the fated change approve;
Then murderous War, with all t e baleful train
    Of vices, that the world triumphant rove,
Shall yield to Peace, and Harmony, and Love;
    Again Aftræa from the fkies defcend,
And ne'er again her dwelling to remove;
    The paffions fierce their dying fury fpend;
And angels o'er our blifs, with fmiles of rapture bend.

*   *   *   *   *   *

*   *   *   *   *   *

Mark avarice firſt, with lean and fallow face,
   And hollow eyes, of red and piercing glare ;
Loofe filthy rags his toil-bent form difgrace,
   And hangs unkempt his foul and matted hair ;
His bofom feels one fole and fordid care,
   Vaft fhining heaps of ufelefs drofs to pile,
Nor would he, from this drofs, a portion fpare,
   For all the joys that bafk in beauty's fmile,
Or e'en the laurel wreath that waits Ambition's toil.

In league with him grofs ignorance is join'd,
   Around whofe head eternal fogs do fwim,
Nathlefs his darknefs can he never find,
   Nor careth for the Sun's enliv'ning beam ;
And tho' athwart the mift it fometimes gleam,
   He fhuts his eyes and will not take the light,
Nor will be waken'd from his ftupid dream ;
   'Twould pity move to fee his wretched plight,
Yet laughs he aye, and feems a moft contented wight.

b

Thefe two here hold an uncontrolled fway,
　　And all before their fordid thrones do bend,
And all devotion at their altars pay ;
　　But whither, Mufe, unbridled doft thou tend,
Nor car'ft unthinking, whom thou doft offend ?
　　Certes, thy folly foon fhall work thee rue
Nor e'er repentance fhall thy rafhnefs mend ;
　　God grant my terrors now may prove untrue,
And thou efcape the fangs of the enraged crew ;

　*　　　*　　　*　　　*　　　*　　　*　　　*
　　*　　　*　　　*　　　*　　　*　　　*

" How hard the heart of proud oppreffive Man,
　" How thick a mift involves his mental eye,
" How doth he mar our gracious Maker's plan,
　" Which to his paffions vile he feeks to ply ;
" He fees your tears, he fees the burfting figh
　" Rack your foft bofoms, yet unmov'd remains,
" Firm as the oak, that rears his head on high,
　" And ftands the monarch of the fubject plains,
" In vain, a tempeft blows, in vain, a deluge rains.

" Ah ! why has bounteous Nature thus fupplied,
 " This ftream exhauftlefs of obedient tears,
" If nought avail, to pour the willing tide ?
 " What ray of hope our dark defpondence cheers,
" Since e'en our faintings, and hyfteric fears,
 " No longer touch the rugged iron breaft
" Of man ? he fteels his heart, he fhuts his ears,
 " To all our prayers however artful dreft ;
" And all our efforts foils, the rod of fway to wreft.

* * * * * *
 * * * * *
* * * * * *

Trembling and flow the modeft maid arofe,
 One hand her fwelling bofom gently preft,
While all her face, with fudden crimfon, glows,
 *And Hope and Fear ufurp, by turns, her breaft ;
So o'er the greenfward, Nature's pleafant veft,
 Now ftreams of light, with gentle waving, ftray,
Now fhades of momentary darknefs reft,
 As flying clouds reveal or hide the ray,
Pour'd from yon golden orb, great regent of the day.

*The following allufion, in one of Mr. Home's tragedies,
appeared to me to unite almoft every excellence,

Awhile fhe paus'd ! expecting filence reign'd ;

 The firft faint accents on her lips expire ;

Again fhe blufh'd ; but foon, frefh courage gain'd,

 Diftinctly fpeaks, and all her fears retire ;

*So when the Zephyrs thrill their airy lyre,

 And wake, with gentle breath, the confcious ftrings,

With gradual fwell, the trembling notes afpire,

 (Sweet as the ftrain the bird of midnight fings,)

Till all the vale, with foft repeated echoes, rings.

—— *Hope and Fear, alternate fway'd his breaft,*
Like light and shade upon a waving field,
Courfing each other, when the flying clouds
Now hide, and now reveal the Sun.

• *Here the analogy is remarkably perfect, not only between*
light and hope, and between darknefs and fear, but between
the rapid fucceffion of light and shade, and the momentary
 nfluences of thofe oppofite emotions ; and at the fame time,
the new image, which is prefented to us, is one of the moft
beautiful and ftriking in nature.
      Stewart's El. Phi. of the H. M.
        page 308, quar· ed.

So when the Zephyrs, &c. *I fincerely beg pardon of*
the Critics, for calling the harp of Æolus the " lyre of
the Zephyrs."

* * * * *
* * * * *

Woman, indeed, may boaſt a right divine,
   From Heav'ns own bounty ſhe derives her claim,
And whilſt I live, ſhall thought and deed of mine,
   Aſſert her rights and vindicate her fame ;
And ever, with loud voice, will I proclaim
   Her as the lawful ſovereign of the ſoul,
And while my veins ſhall warm this vital flame,
   E'en from the Northern to the Southern pole,
Unwearied will I try to ſpread her juſt control.

Nor you, ye fair, too proud, diſdain the aid,
   Which now I offer, with a heart ſincere,
Nor ſcorn the poet, who has thus aſſay'd,
   O'er vain revolting Man your ſway to rear, ;
But to his verſes lend attentive ear,
   And with approving ſmile receive the lay,
Thus from his breaſt diſſolve that icy fear,
   Which binds the Muſe, long ſtruggling to the day,
Like ſpringing lark, ſhe mounts, and tunes her carol gay.

Nor heed of witlings the malicious fneer,
   Nor credit give, to their affertion bafe,
That fatire's hideous features would appear,
   If torn the painted mask, that hides her face,
That even now, thofe features they can trace,
   So ill the mask of praife is fitted on ;
A wretch were I, unworthy of your grace,
   If this were true ; I own, I truft, that none
Will credit lies, more glaring than the noon-day Sun.

What ! I the fex deride, who round my heart
   The filken cords of love fo ftrong have twin'd,
That from this durance I may never part,
   Nor thefe fweet chains, with all my force unbind ;
To truth's refulgent light, I ween, moft blind
   Is he, who fuch grofs folly dare maintain,
Beyond redrefs, corrupted is his mind,
   Who could, with lie so foul, his confcience ftain ;
Of fuch low cenfurers, now fcorn I to complain ;

     *   *   *   *   *
       *   *   *   *   *

Ah ! who would ſtill the pulſe of youthly mind,
    That with the hope of fame doth reſtleſs beat ;
Who with grave counſel, or reproach unkind,
    Would quench the flame of that celeſtial heat,
That warms the boſoms of the good and great,
    And forces to contemn each ſorrow'd care,
And ſhun the haunts where vice and ſhame do meet ;
    And yet I ween, there ſtill are men who dare,
This warmth and virtuous zeal, with madneſs to compare.

I grant, if lucre be the end of life,
    And all our thoughts and cares ſhould thither tend ;
That ſhould we mix in ſuch ignoble ſtrife,
    And for ſo mean, ſo vile a prize contend ;
Then muſt the lore of prudence all be ken'd,
    And ſunk the light of the ſupernal ray ;
Our ſinful nature by degrees to mend,
    And climb the ſteep, where, midſt eternal day,
Fair virtue ſits enthron'd, no more muſt we aſſay.

Behold the flaves, whom avarice fubdues,
 And drives, and goads, to unremitting toil ;
Mark, with what ftern delight the Tyrant views,
 Their bootlefs labor, and exults the while
The wretches fuffer from his cruel guile.
 For fplendid vifions ftill enchain the fight
And mock their wifhes, and their efforts foil ;
 What tho' the fiend their golden harvefts blight,
Deluded and enthrall'd, they drudge from morn to night.

Belov'd of Heav'n, ye facred band, I hail,
 Whofe virtuous breafts, the love of truth infpires ;
Tho' Malice, Envy, fhould your worth affail,
 Tho' Poverty confine your large defires,
Your conftant purpofe ne'er Misfortune tires ;
 Nor Woe extinguifhes the holy flame,
That whence it comes, ftill Heavenward afpires.
 Ah ! why fhould I reprefs the hope that Fame,
Where yours fhe blazons full, may mark my humble name.

And hail ! ye mighty mafters of the fong ,
   Who e'en to thrilling rapture wake the foul ;
'To you the powers of magic fpell belong,
   For as ye lift, ye bear from pole to pole
The fpirit rapt ; now thundering torrents roll,
   And dafh, and foam, impetuous to the plain——
Have fcenes of Eden on my fenfes ftole ?
   Do Seraphs breathe that foft, entrancing ftrain ?
Ah ! do not ftill the lyre, refound thofe notes again.

But when diffolves the fervid fancy's dream,
   To real life unwilling we return.
How vain all fublunary cares we deem !
   How fcorn the limits of this tranfient bourne !
Miftaken youth ! thy facred duties learn,
   And ftrive to fill the part, that God has giv'n,
Tho' far more perfect blifs thy bofom yearn,
   Know, 'tis our trial here that leads to heav'n,
He, that in floth repines, fhall never be forgiv'n.

And now my wearied hand, and wearied mind,
   Demand repofe, and further toil refufe ;
But fhould Apollo round my temples bind
   A garland, drench'd in pure caftalian dews,
The guerdon fair would vigour frefh infufe ;
   Perhaps, embolden'd by the voice of praife,
The Mufe might dare fome nobler theme to chufe,
   The which adorn'd, a deathlefs name fhall raife,
O'er Time's unbounded fea, with conftant flame, to blaze.

CONCLUDING SONNET.

Farewell! bleſt ſcenes, where Fancy pours her day,
 And ſheds a ſofter, more romantic light ;
 Where Beauty's living forms entrance the ſight,
And ſweeteſt muſic warbles from each ſpray ;
Scenes, where the lonely bard is wont to ſtray,
 And as your charms his warmeſt ſoul excite,
 Paints what he ſees in colors ever bright.
With ſlow reluctant ſtep, I ſhun your ſway,
Bleſt ſcenes, farewell! now ſolemn duties call ;
 Now muſt I mingle in the worldly ſtrife,
Of anxious care, of ceaſeleſs toil the thrall ;
 And yet, ſhould Providence extend my life,
Once more emerging from the tranſient gloom,
I'll quaff your ſprings, and cull your faireſt bloom.

FINIS.

ERRATA.

Page 4, line 4, read amœni—5, 11, where—6, 6, fœnum—8, camœnis—10, 4, præbere —12, 3, promittere—14, 10, quæ— 0, 10, comœdus—2 , 14, lævis—30, 5, recens—38, 6, villicus—40, 12, infelix—41, 12, length—42, 3, Asturi—8, præclarum —43, 13, dome—44, 3, Circensibus—13, fenestre 111, 7, unfetter'd—120, 1, not—125, 7, were—126, 3, lead—128, 2, unnumber'd—131, 8, hope—142, 7, debilitatos.

ADDITIONAL ERRATA.

Page 11	Line 8	for county read	Country.
25	10	when	where.
31	14	Pander's	Panders'.
61	15	breath	breathe.
68	5	when	where.
72	22	arrigare	arrigere.
73	12	and	or
do	15	you	a
71	19	strangely	strongly
96	18	inking	sinking
93	22	somn	somno
101	4	strains	strain
115	19	signs	sighs
119	4	summer's	summer
120	9	vain	vein
do	14	dispair	despair
144	1	Insert a comma after flocks.	
160	5	Insert a semicolon after year.	

Page 165	Line 7 for	while it	read willing
169	8	rest	list
171	2	where	when
172	3	and	all
do	8	day	day's
183	1	thus	then
187.	6	sorrow'd	sordid
189	7	far	for
191	7 change the period after " bright" to a comma.
do.	8 change the comma after "sway" to a period.

A line from Pope's " Temple of Fame" inserted in the last Poem, has been inadvertently printed without the marks of quotation.

32101 064068024